THE FACE OF THE DEEP

Works by Thomas Farber

Tales for the Son of My Unborn Child

Rag Theatre
(with the photographs of Nacio Brown)

Who Wrote the Book of Love?

Hazards to the Human Heart

Too Soon to Tell

Curves of Pursuit

Compared to What?

Learning to Love It

On Water

The Price of the Ride

Through a Liquid Mirror
(with the photographs of Wayne Levin)

Compressions: A Second Helping

THE FACE OF THE DEEP

Thomas Farber

Mercury House

San Francisco

Published in the United States of America by Mercury House, San Francisco, California, a nonprofit publishing company devoted to the free exchange of ideas and guided by a dedication to literary values.

Library of Congress Cataloging-in-Publication Data:
Farber, Thomas, 1944–
The face of the deep / Thomas Farber. — 1st ed.
p. cm.
ISBN 1-56279-112-5 (acid-free paper)
1. Farber, Thomas, 1944–   —Journeys—Pacific Area. 2. Authors, American—20th century—Biography. 3. Pacific Area—Description and travel. 4. Aquatic sports—Pacific Area. 5. Pacific Area—Civilization. I. Title.
PS3556.A64Z4655   1998
813'.54—DC21   98-24332
[B]   CIP

5 4 3 2 1
FIRST EDITION

To the memory of Hsu Yu (1908–1980)
&
for Black Oak, Cody's, Moe's, Serendipity

In the beginning God created the heavens and the earth. The earth was without form and void, and darkness was upon the face of the deep ...

—from the Hebrew Bible,
the First Book of Moses

The souvenir must be removed from its context in order to serve as a trace of it, but it must also be restored through narrative and/or reverie. What it is restored to is not an "authentic," that is, a native, context of origin but an imaginary context of origin whose chief subject is a projection of the possessor's childhood.

—Susan Stewart, *On Longing*

Everything deep loves a mask ...

—Friedrich Nietzsche, *Beyond Good and Evil*

Contents

Introduction

A decade and more ago, back in Berkeley after yet another long stay in Hawai'i, at my desk trying to reconcile aquatic and writerly obsessions, I received a call from a friend in publishing. The miracle of corporate lines: a familiar voice from New York at no apparent cost to either of us. In the course of our conversation, she asked what I was working on. "A book about water," I answered. Intentional deadpan: I was trying to deflect the question. A book exists only in the telling, after all. It was also true I didn't yet have even a strategy for what I'd be trying to achieve. Responding to the obvious impracticability of so vast a topic, my friend retorted, "Oh, and then a book about fire." Fair enough, I thought.

As it happened, *On Water* (1994) proved to be an effort to "read" water—to find words for what was right before my eyes—as well an appraisal of how others had read it. The book completed, however, I found myself still engaged by (warm) oceans: unlikely that for me there'd be a fire next time. (It was Robert Frost who, after considering ice as a force of destruction, came out in favor of fire.)

Water and writing. Though natural antagonists in some ways—there's little verbal wit in the ocean (though much irony and play)—they also complement each other: water of course elicits deep human response, some of it in words; as Kafka argued, writing is the ax to break the frozen sea within. (And, poet John Keats wrote, "Which is the best of Shakespeare's plays? I mean in what mood and with what accompaniment do you like the sea best?") Also, both writers and oceans know well the conjuring of reflection and refraction—think of Joseph Conrad's "Mirror of the Sea."

Following publication of *On Water,* I continued my Pacific travels, kept being saved by (even the most threatening) waves in the way Roger Payne suggests humans have been saved by whales. But as I sustained my focus on water and islands, it became ever more obvious to me that I was (also/nonetheless/therefore) drowning in memories: describing the watery present inevitably led me to the past. Thus, writing these pages, I've tried to yield to that set of concomitant realities—those simultaneous zones of time. And, where possible, to make a virtue of them. Doing this has also been part of a larger hunger, to be awake to the complexities of the life I've been living, to acknowledge and find the words to articulate—to sing!—these anomalies, these intricacies, these at-least-partial truths.

Completing the voyage that was this book, I want to acknowledge gifts that enabled a safe return: from Sara Bershtel, Bob Crane, Kim Darwin, Gavan Daws, Tom Drazin, Dan Duane, Tony Dubovsky, Ella Ellis, Epi Enari, Jim Houston, Vilsoni Hereniko, Fran Kaufman, Helen Lang, Reagan Louie, Paul Lyons, Joseph Matthews, Pat Matsueda, Stephen Mitchell, Fred Miller, Kennedy Moore, Steve Moser, Louise Quayle, Tia Reber, Stephen Rosenberg, Frank Stewart, Terry Strauss, and Michael White. In addition, the Center for Documentary Photography at Duke University, through its Dorothea Lange–Paul Taylor Prize, underwrote a South Pacific trip, and a National Endowment for the Arts fellowship in creative nonfiction made possible more water time and travel. My thanks also to Mercury House for the *aloha* of its commitment to a rich diversity of written voices, and to the Overbrook Foundation for supporting that commitment.

Finally, literary agent Ellen Levine ... In our nearly twenty-five years of collaboration, she has yet to suggest that, as writer, I try in any way to be what I am not. A great gift, such acceptance, given real-world imperatives here on the material plane.

Thomas Farber
Berkeley, California
Honolulu, Hawai'i

THE FACE OF THE DEEP

Isla del Coco

§

First light, searching out 5°33'
north latitude, 8°3' west longitude. Dieseling the Pacific, three
hundred miles west of Costa Rica. A fragment of Isla del Coco
(a.k.a. Cocos Island) emerging from heavy cloud cover, rising and
falling in the deep blue. Surrounded by strong currents, not part
of an archipelago, often obscured—historically, an elusive place.
Boobies riding wind swell off the prow; mist; frigate birds soaring
out of sight; one rainbow, another; dolphins surfing the bow
wave—all this in focus for a moment only to disappear, dissipate,
then again to appear, cohere.

Sheltered waters after thirty-five hours hobbyhorsing in the
swell: pitching, veering, dropping. Rocking, the only lullaby a
mewing *moo* as one dry-heaves. Finally achieving the conclusion
that the goal of being human is compassion. Simultaneously realizing this to be not epiphany but self-pity. (That great ecotourist
Charles Darwin, aboard the *Beagle* in the Galapagos, not far south
of here, never overcame his seasickness.)

Land ho, this remote volcanic island some five by two miles.

Rugged coastline uninhabited except for a few Costa Rican National Park rangers, densely covered steep cliffs how Babylon's Nebuchadnezzer might have envisioned his hanging gardens. And, with twenty-five feet of precipitation each year—rain forest, gorges, waterfalls, ravines, cloud forest, ridges, streams. In such humid tropical isolation, vegetable fertility: many endemic insects, birds, lizards, plants (that is, found only here). This seclusion and clean water also perfect, from the seventeenth to early nineteenth centuries, for pirates—Cocos one of the world's most famous treasure islands. And, recently, given its phenomenal profusion of marine life, an underwater Mecca for divers.

Our dive boat: two morning dives, one afternoon dive, a night dive. Again and again suiting up, checking tank pressure, into the Zodiac rubber dinghies toward yet another offshore pinnacle. The surface now glassy, now a pulsing swell. Sometimes, underwater, a strong current or "wind," or a sudden upwelling of colder water. Often ascending to encounter rain at the interface of the (allegedly) terrestrial world. Hard rain, harder, spigot being opened, drops detonating, sky gray, clouds obscuring the island as the diver pops up through the liquid mirror, again achieves uncompressed air, bobs like a cork.

Sharks. "Shark-infested waters," divemaster Mario Arroyo shouts as the Zodiac approaches another underwater pinnacle. Everyone grins. There are always whitetip reef sharks when we dive, scores of them. They're gray, slender, with short blunt snouts, about five feet long, splotches of white on the foreward dorsal fin and upper lobe of the tail, as if daubed with a large brush, carelessly, without concern for straight lines. This detail comes to me only after a number of dives, only after the whitetip sharks have begun to seem like reef fish, so common are they. Sometimes swimming toward us, occasionally hunting, a group of them surrounding some fish trapped in the rocks, but generally, being nocturnal creatures, lying at rest on sandy bottoms or rocky ledges. Determinedly motionless, moving only when we come too close, reluctantly, like cats disturbed enough by the children to grudgingly give up their place at the hearth.

The whitetips become profane, then: what elsewhere would have compelled one's full attention here is soon ordinary. But not the hammerheads, some ten feet long, head flattened and extended to both sides, an eye far out on either edge. These "lateral extensions" making a width equal to a quarter of the shark's total length. Such a streamlined forward wing perhaps aiding locomotion, increasing lift and maneuverability, or improving sight and smell by spreading the sense organs. The eyes, from the point of view of the diver, enormous, distended. Mouth relatively small, compared to other sharks', a jack-o-lantern leer. The hammerheads frequently moving with a kind of strutting wag, as if hinged in the middle, the whole torso and head wrenching one way, the rest of the body the other, giving their approach an (unsettling) abruptness. Or, startled, they disappear in an instant, making one realize just how suddenly they could reappear …

Often a hammerhead passes, then several, but at a distance, in the murk, the gloaming. Fifty feet away or more. Only after several days of diving, again down deep to begin and then up a little to crouch in the rocks, holding on in the strong current, do we see a school, a squadron of hammerheads. Perhaps sixty of them, very close, groups of two and three and then a cluster of twenty, many whitetips circling below us, and also a large cloud of jacks just hanging there. But the hammerheads: though we have been searching for them, waiting for them, their sudden relentless proximity and sheer numbers—and impact of that silhouette on the cerebral cortex, message imprinted eons ago—spins me into adrenelin overdrive. Hyperventilating, one hears oneself exhaling hard, a river of bubbles shooting up, then sucking more air as one tries to take in the hammerheads just overhead. Suddenly—don't let the children read this—feeling like the bomber's turret gunner in some World War II movie. Bandits at one o'clock, at two, at five, oh sweet Jesus.

And then, just as the last group of hammerheads passes, one turns, fast: something very large in the peripheral vision. Which clarifies itself as Bob from Wausau, Wisconsin, a hefty and good-natured man, two hundred and seventy-five pounds plus weight belt plus tank effortlessly suspended there at eighty feet, neutrally buoyant, his fingers interlaced in the diver's Zen position, in this instant the incarnation of an aquatic Bhudda. Having seen it all and smiling broadly, giving two thumbs up and then a double *okay* sign.

Back in the Zodiac, a large ray at the surface, then several dolphins approaching, dorsal fins cutting water like butter. Wired. "*Hay muchos tiburones,*" I tell José, the boatman. Hammerheads, yes, and by God I have been hammered. Ball-peened; sledged. More than I can process: after lunch, totally spent, I sleep.

～⌒〜

Yet another dive. So much marine life. Sensory overload: where to begin? With the many rays, wings rippling? With that turtle, those Moorish idols, that silky shark? This dive, we're near Wafer Bay, coming up to eighty feet, and encounter a school of silvery bigeye jacks, one to two feet in length. A school? A thundercloud, a tornado, thousands of jacks, the mass incredibly thick and dense, a slowly rotating vortex, then two vortexes. There's no question what's next: though fearful of causing it to disperse, one enters the wheeling cluster of bodies, of eyes. Blessedly, however, it persists, one is surrounded by, engulfed in, it. Something about this rotating shape hauntingly familiar, evoking the kind of spiraling that marks the absolutely essential. Say, for instance, creation of the galaxies.

Not far off Cocos Island, eighty feet below sea level, in the vortex of the jacks, eyes focusing and refocusing in the air pocket behind my mask, trying to take in what I'm seeing, I'm on the verge of tears. More water.

～

So much time below the surface, one not surprisingly begins to read humans in terms of marine life. Echoes: not only did we come from the sea, but vertebrates evolved from gill-respiring fish that developed lungs well before they emerged from the water. Some came ashore with the same arm and leg bones as land animals. We are, in fact, merely "highly advanced fishes," icthyologist John A. Long argues.

Consider our dive boat, then, in piscine terms: the divers as, say, a school, individuals perhaps being picked off, but the collective persisting. (There's the hoary diver's joke about what to do when a shark attacks: "Stab your buddy and swim away.")

Or read the divers not as a school but as different marine species. Big fish, little fish. Seeing these creatures—from eel to tuna to shark to urchin to Moorish idol—comes the question, What niche do you imagine yourself occupying? "I wouldn't want to be a bait fish," says a diver from L.A., perhaps influenced by residing in a place where people are so aware of who's at the top of the food chain, a city that seems to require physical perfection even as it attracts both predators and remoras (remoras having sucking disks by which they attach themselves to larger creatures). This fellow, by the way, a proponent of natural living, reads breast augmentation as "good for self-esteem."

Still, for any of us on board, surveying the inexorable marine options ... what, really, are the available totems, analogies? Or is this a too-human misreading, a hunger for a world defined by our (limited) moral vision? William Blake wrote,

> How do you know but ev'ry Bird that cuts the airy way
> Is an immense world of delight, clos'd by your senses five?

Or, the Voice in the whirlwind demands of Job, what do *you* know about the Creation? Were you there (as Stephen Mitchell renders it) "while the morning stars burst out singing/and the angels shouted for joy?" This is also, of course, the Creator who "stopped the waters,/as they issued gushing from the womb," who "swaddled the sea in shadows" and "closed it in with barriers and set its boundaries ..." As opposed to the Genesis myth, at the heart of this Creation, Mitchell argues, there is "indestructible power" and "indestructible joy" but also "the destructive Shiva-aspect of God" in a "continuum of nature, which runs seamlessly from angel to beast." For Mitchell, Blake had it right when he argued that there are "portions of eternity too great for the eye of man."

Imponderables: in this section of Job the Voice also demands, "have you walked through the depths of the ocean/or dived to the floor of the sea?" To this particular (rhetorical) question, we on board happen to be able to answer in the affirmative. Nonetheless … as below, so above. Day ending, the black frigate birds still wheel, surfing thermals without any apparent motion of their six-foot wingspans, occasionally opening or closing their forked tails for better gliding or stalling (able even to soar all night), sometimes plunging with incredible speed to snatch flying fish or squid from the surface, or to harass boobies with their scimitar-tipped beaks, forcing them to disgorge their catch. Klepto-parasites, the frigate birds (and, for good measure, cannibals), well adapted, it seems, for the interface of air, land, and water.

Four AM, bilge pumping, boat tugging at anchor, ship's company sleeping soundly as … the dead. Rolling out of my berth, heading up to check the stars. At the stern, finding Jupiter close to the waxing moon. And just below, at the surface, unmistakable sounds of the chase, fish jumping, over and over again, like stones skipping, this constant motion, then suddenly the fin and torso of a shark.

Head throbbing from too much diving: a constant banging on the anvil of the left inner ear. Demands of submersing: having to equalize pressure, of course; and having to make peace with the presence of so many hunters, hunted. Several feet down, the mayhem of pursuit continues. Evoking a Philip Larkin line:

> … *crouching below*
> *Extinction's alp, the old fools, never perceiving*
> *How near it is.*

In our terrestrial lives, most of us are exempted now from participating in the chase—select predators do our killing for us—and the millions of our own kind who die annually do so mostly out of sight. Not so for the species here, however.

Divemaster Javier, finishing his watch, passes by, smiles. I marvel: a determinedly positive spirit, this man. *"Como está, Don Tomás?"* Javier sings out. I respond as he's taught me: *"Pura vida."* The Costa Rican affirmative—"super." But also literally true in this place of such powerful esentials. *Pura vida:* pure life. The proximity of incessant death notwithstanding.

∿

Time for a respite from water. Cocos is uninhabited except for the few rangers at their small station at Wafer Bay. Crossing Rio Genio in the humid heat, river cool and clear, one is almost immediately scrambling up steep, muddy slopes toward Cerro Iglesias (elevation some two thousand feet). This is luxuriant premontane rain forest, with small sparrowlike birds staying very close, inquisitive. Trees covered with epiphytes—aerophytes(!), plants growing on other plants—such as bromeliads. Soon, without sound, more water: a misting rain. And then a whirring. Just behind, a white espiritu santo tern. Hovering, almost translucent wings fluttering as it emits, in odd contrast, nasal clunking sounds.

Walking on. Long since, soaked, sweating. Trees dripping, ground saturated, but most of the rain itself deflected by the canopy. Above, nesting frigate birds scream, clap, cackle, squeal, some with enormous long black wings outspread. And below, a group of feral pigs, descendants of animals introduced, with goats and cats, by whalers and pirates several centuries ago.

Later, back at the river, washing off—the muddy descent was not always on foot—then exploring a cave near the rocky shore. This one, it seems, was enlarged by a treasure hunter who spent years on Cocos. Treasure: using Cocos as his headquarters in the late seventeenth century, English pirate Edward Davis, emulating

Sir Francis Drake's earlier exploits, raided the coast of New Spain. Though later amnestied by James II, Davis apparently never made it back to Cocos to recover what he'd hidden. Life on Davis's *Bachelor's Delight* was documented by William Dampier and Lionel Wafer in journals that were bestsellers at the time and source material for writers including Daniel Defoe.

In the early nineteenth century, pirate "Bloody" Benito Bonito, having taken Spanish treasure, divided and buried it on Cocos. Or so it's told. In the same era, renegade English Navy captain Bennett Graham of the *Devonshire* buried *his* Spanish booty on Cocos, according to his companion Mary Welch, who survived being transported to the penal colony in Tasmania, later returning to Cocos to lead an (unsuccessful) hunt.

Meanwhile, there was the fabled treasure of Lima. According to writer Christopher Weston Knight (whose father, Julian, also published a book about Cocos), the Spanish viceroy, fearing the attack of rebel colonists in 1821, entrusted it all to Captain William Thompson of the *Mary Dear*. The cargo, Knight writes, included "a solid gold, gem-encrusted, life-sized image of the Virgin Mary." Killing the Peruvian guards, (the hitherto trustworthy) Captain Thompson headed for … Cocos where he, yes, buried his riches. Subsequently captured by the Peruvians, Thompson did or did not lead them back to Cocos, did or did not pass on a map to a Canadian named Keating. Who, later leading an expedition to Cocos, apparently found at least a hint of some treasure, though, in 1894, his widow found nothing at all. (According to Theon Wright, this Captain *Jack* Thompson had a long history of piracy, was in fact the same Thompson who once sailed under Benito Bonito; his boat was the Nova Scotia bark *Mary Deer*, not *Dear*;

and Thompson took his Peruvian plunder in 1835, the spoils of 1821 having gone off in the *Black Witch* under a Captain Henry Smith. You can see the problems for treasure hunters.)

All of which set in motion what commentators term "hundreds" of expeditions on Cocos, a number surely as imprecise as the alleged value of the alleged treasures. But there were many, one of them the voyage of Sir Malcolm Campbell, a racecar driver, who in 1925 had in hand "the clue to the *Mary Dear* treasure," received "from the most reliable sources possible ..." Sir Malcolm found only ants and sweltering heat on his first try, but returned in 1935, having issued a prospectus and sold shares (in Cocos Island Treasure Limited) to finance the trip. Still, apparently, no booty.

German-born sailor August Gissler, however, seems to have most deserved to find treasure, given his nearly twenty years on Cocos, beginning in 1889. Fate marked out Gissler as surely as it put the hot-tempered Oedipus on the road his father was traveling. A Portuguese shipmate let Gissler copy a map said to belong to a man who'd sailed with Benito Bonito; and years later, in Hawai'i, Gissler saw an old beachcomber's chart. Cocos again. Which led Gissler eventually to Boston to a son-in-law of Keating-the-Canadian (thus connected to Captain Jack or Captain William Thompson, thus connected to Benito Bonito), and to years digging on Cocos. At one point, a naturalized Costa Rican, Gissler was appointed governor of the island.

In 1925, a New York Zoological Society oceanographic ship stopped at Cocos. Back in New York, expedition member Ruth Rose sought out Gissler, who was by then living in an apartment near the roaring trains of the El, "remembering tree ferns under a tropical moon, while he watches the flicker of an electric sign ..."

The scientists had visited Gissler's abandoned settlement at Wafer Bay, seen his decaying house. Now, Ruth Rose met a "big man, straight and upstanding as a youth, with a white beard that covered his chest, bright blue eyes that could twinkle or glower, and the shipshape trimness that speaks of seafaring ..." Ten years later, believing he owned Cocos, Gissler died, bequeathing part of the island to oceanographer William Beebe, director of that Zoological Society expedition.

Treasure and its tropes: deathbed confessions; maps; fundraising. Tunnels; caves; shards. Portents. August Gissler once found a palm tree on Cocos on which had been carved, in English, *The Bird is Gone.* Signifying what, Gissler must have wondered. Must have agonized.

Cocos. People still come for treasure, park rangers now quick to shoo them away. But such dreams die hard. In Truman Capote's *In Cold Blood,* murderers Perry Smith and Richard Hickock fantasize about running a fishing boat, though neither has ever been to sea. But Perry reads adventure magazines, has information. "'No fooling, Dick,' Perry said. 'This is authentic. I've got a map. I've got the whole history. It was buried there back in 1821—Peruvian bullion, jewelry. Sixty million dollars—that's what they say it's worth. Even if we didn't find all of it, even if we found only some of it— Are you with me, Dick?'"

Real or not, treasures live on, reverberate, have their own (long) atomic half-life. In 1968, I sailed down the coast of California, crewing for a skipper who, divorce impending, was selling the vessel he and his wife had built. Years later, I learned that this man's father claimed he found treasure on Cocos Island. Perhaps he really had.

⟶

And meet it is, that over these sea-pastures, wide-rolling watery prairies and Potters' Fields of all four continents, the waves should rise and fall; for here, millions of mixed shades and shadows, drowned dreams, somnambulisms, reveries; all that we call lives and souls, lie dreaming, dreaming still; tossing like slumberers in their beds; the ever-rolling waves but made so by their restlessness.

—Herman Melville, *Mardi*

The currents are sobering: one recalls those Japanese drift divers in Palau, missing their boat rendezvous; never seen again. And then there's the danger of nitrogen in the blood—"Getting bent," divers call it, insouciantly. Nearest recompression chamber more than thirty-five hours away. One can also worry about ear infections—two divers on board succumb, are unable to submerge. All this begging the question put to me by an almost-twelve-year-old upon my return. "Tom, did you carry a bangstick?" (*Bangstick*—a euphemism equipped with a bullet that explodes on impact.) My answer: "No, though a man I met, a divemaster a few years ago at Cocos, says he had to use his bangstick there, killed a Galapagos shark."

The unspoken guidelines, surely worth making explicit in an era of such determined (and unilateral?) reconciliation between humans and some other species:

- Sharks around Cocos are well fed, given the abundance of fish;
- Humans are not (yet) in their normal diet, being seldom seen, and not of particular interest unless bleeding or close to fish that are bleeding;
- Sharks appear not to like scuba divers' bubbles or the

flash of cameras. May even, in fact, be described as skittish, easily spooked.

- One stays close to pinnacles, avoiding blue—deep, open—water where one is a clear target and where the shark has more room to maneuver or, worse, to accelerate up from below;

- The hammerheads come in to these sea mounts during the day after feeding on fish and squid at night, often miles away. To rest? To mate? Or perhaps simply to be cleaned of parasites by small angelfish.

- Thus, whitetip reef sharks and hammerheads, at least near the pinnacles, may rarely pose a threat. With silkies and Galapagos sharks, however, not to mention oceanic whitetips, the rule is to get out of the water, fast, if the shark starts to look "interested."

One night, three very experienced divers on board see Galapagos sharks near the ship and banter each other into a dive to film them. Though intending to stay near the surface, they soon descend—are lured down?—to sixty feet, where several Galapagos sharks suddenly rematerialize. There, one of them begins to menace the diver carrying the video camera, which occasions some impressive footage of the shark's repeated attack approach. Though all three divers make it up into the boat, the diver with the camera says he'll never risk such a dive again.

As our industrialized species learns more about them, it's clear that many sharks aren't as dangerous as they seem—whatever alarm bell their gestalt triggers in the unconscious—or that the dangers can be minimized. It was the great Hawaiian waterman Duke Kahanamoku who said of sharks, "I don't bother them, they don't bother me." And it's true, I've seen Fijian villagers in the lagoon, nonchalantly spear fishing in the presence of, say, reef sharks. Nonetheless, I also know that surfers have been attacked recently by tiger sharks in Hawai'i, though there reef fish are now depleted, thousands of humans are in the water daily, and surfers linger at the surface (looking from below like turtles or rays). It's also true, however, that even in Hawai'i shark attacks are far less frequent than, for instance, car wrecks or suicide attempts.

Nevertheless, to spend time in the water with sharks, even at Cocos, may be what my mother wryly termed "living as if." She herself had tuberculosis as a young woman, but survived; lived through two world wars, the extermination of European Jewry, the Korean War, the Vietnam War; saw in her circle the normal array of disease, madness, accidents, bad luck, misery. Is it any wonder that several of my mother's last books were survivor stories? Noah, the ark, those left-behind beasts. Thus my mother seemed to mean that we insistently live each day *as if* life will go on, as if we can count on being here tomorrow; as if we can count on being ourselves to be here tomorrow. As if the sharks accept the terms we divers propose.

⁓

In the Zodiac, divers surfacing as air runs low, there are words: a naming of what one saw. Delicate business, one's saga, since other divers may have been at a different depth or spot, may have been unable to make out what was only fifty or seventy-five feet away. May not fully appreciate the elation of others. Or may prefer silence, trying to describe to themselves what it was they saw. Struggling to articulate the ineffable, even exultation or wonderment being (strangely?) difficult to express. Even having "gotten" a glimpse of what you came so far for. How name, how retain, it?

There's also the human impulse to share, prove, possess, display. Nearly each diver, emerging, before coming aboard the Zodiac hands up a camera, most of them costing thousands of dollars. There's a darkroom on the ship, film developed overnight—and video of course can be seen immediately. Thus almost instant metacommunication transpires, a viewing of simulacra of what we saw to … see what we saw? At times, the images themselves appear to be the goal.

To the "skin" or "free" diver—using only mask/fins/snorkel, such empowering tools—scuba may seem costly, gear-intensive, evoking jousting's armor and retainers. Add to this the breakdown of photographic equipment in salt water, inevitable tinkering, repair. Late in our stay at Cocos, Gary, a land developer from the Midwest, finally decides to dive without his camera. "I'm tired of seeing it all through a viewfinder," he tells us, albeit still ambivalent.

Being in nature here seems inextricably interwined with recording experience, a pursuit at least as all-consuming as, say, adolescent sex. I myself note this on one of my many trips below deck to turn on my—laptop!—computer, eager to compose a version of our voyage. Afraid of "losing" it. Meanwhile waiting impatiently for photographer Wayne Levin's black-and-white photos (which he won't develop until we return home).

Amazed, nonetheless, by the collective documentation being

done by these professional and skilled amateur divers, one day I think of physicist Werner Heisenberg's Uncertainty Principle: to observe is to disturb; there's no way to see something without affecting the thing seen. Perhaps the issue of technology is a red herring, so to speak. French philosopher Pascal, a cool eye *his* aperture, argued that we wouldn't cross oceans for "the sheer pleasure of seeing things we could never hope to describe to others," or "if it meant never talking about it."

～

Trying to take stock of the miraculous. For instance, where am I when I'm in the water? Including oceans, seas, glaciers, lakes, and rivers, water covers about three quarters of our planet. Flatten some peaks and you have one world-wide ocean about a mile and a half deep. In the Biblical flood, the "waters prevailed so mightily upon the earth that all the high mountains under the whole heaven were covered; the waters prevailed above the mountains, covering them fifteen cubits deep." But the deep I'm in, here at Cocos? How take its measure?

Miracles and water. Jesus, Matthew wrote, learning that John the Baptist had been beheaded, withdrew "to a lonely place apart." This was at the Sea of Galilee, a lake, actually. Tear- or pear-shaped, some seven by thirteen miles, through which the Jordan River still flows. There Jesus transformed five loaves and two fish, which fed "about five thousand men, besides women and children." Later, Jesus "made the disciples get into the boat and go before him to the other side ..." while "he went up into the hills by himself to pray." By evening, the boat "was many furlongs distant from the land, beaten by the waves; for the wind was against them. And in the fourth watch of the night he came to them, walking on the sea. But when the disciples saw him walking on the sea, they were terrified, saying, 'It is a ghost!' and they cried out for fear. But immediately he spoke to them, saying, 'Take heart, it is I …'

"And Peter answered him, 'Lord, if it is you, bid me come to you on the water.' He said, 'Come.' So Peter got out of the boat and walked on the water and came to Jesus, but when he saw the wind, he was afraid, and beginning to sink he cried out, 'Lord, save me.' Jesus immediately reached out his hand and caught him, saying to him, 'O man of little faith, why did you doubt?'"

The Sea of Galilee is near the current cease-fire line with Syria, at the foot of the Golan heights, seven hundred feet below the level of the Mediterranean. Drawn to its mild climate—hot summers, a brief rain-winter—and fertile soil, people have lived here for thousands of years. According to the *Encyclopaedia Britannica,* fifteenth edition, the local winds "generally alternate daily, especially in the summer, blowing onshore in the morning and offshore at night. During the winter violent winds occasionally [create] storms on the lake." Finally, because of mineral deposits the lake is quite salty. Not, of course, generally salty enough for walking.

Miracles. *Take heart … Lord, save me.* The fear of drowning even agnostics have experienced. Jesus reaching out. Stilling the waters. Calming the sea.

(Water and our need for the miraculous. Dr. Bernie Seigel, surgeon and author– of *Peace, Love and Healing,* etc.– reasons that God is "'creative intelligence'" and that there is a "loving intelligence" in all matter. For instance, Dr. Siegel says, consider that when you freeze liquids they become more dense, heavier, then sink. But not water, the molecules of which move apart as temperature falls, making it less dense: ice floats. "What would happen to life on Earth," Dr. Siegel asks, "if everything froze from the bottom up? … Where would the fish go? The life in the oceans would die. Water would stop flowing."

That ice so felicitously defies the laws of physics is for Dr. Siegel a sign of divine intelligence. Perhaps, perhaps, but, unhappily, only because he says so. That is, here we're in the domain of faith, not logic.)

～

Water closed over my head; I said, "I am lost."

—Book of Lamentations, 3:54

Doing yet another back roll off the Zodiac, palm against mask. Heading down to, say, one hundred ten feet, equalizing pressure over and again during the descent. Waiting at the bottom for one's buddy, time for a quick look around. And up. Such a long, long way. "Drowning," Sheldon Nuland writes, is "a form of asphyxia in which the mouth and nostrils are occluded by water." (*Asphyxia:* a lack of oxygen and excess of carbon dioxide in the blood. *Occlude:* to close.)

A drowning person struggles, holds his breath. Soon, however, "the air passages all the way down into the lung become obstructed by water." A vomiting reflex may be triggered. There's an initial reflex spasm of the larynx when water first enters the airway, but then "the decreasing blood oxygen relaxes the spasm and water rushes in," the so-called terminal gasp. "A lifeless human body," Nuland notes, "is heavier than water, and the head is its densest part."

In our group, no drownings, merely some ear infections, leaving several divers unable to submerge. As for the rest of us, as son of a doctor I diagnose a collective exhaustion after our collective exhilaration, part of which seems to be a profound sustained overtaxing of the emotions. The clinical term for which is …?

～

Context, context. Cetacean specialist Roger Payne, by nature a meliorist, now appears to find inevitable the imminent demise of large marine creatures due to the poisonous chemicals we're pouring into the ocean. And oceanographer Sylvia Earle, hardly an extremist, warns that we may be overharvesting fish to the point of extinction. Sky's falling? Sea's dying? Where to locate Cocos in all this? Is it merely a remnant of an already lost world? Despite the commitment in Costa Rica to national parks, are they merely Potemkin villages, only facade? Commercial fishing is banned within a nine-mile radius of Cocos, sports-fishing within a five-mile radius. Even so, will long-liners, poaching, and shark finning leave the area a wasteland? Jean-Michel Cousteau has spoken in support of an endowment to help protect Cocos. But even if Cocos is successfully insulated, will it be more than a kind of living diorama? Virtual ocean? One diver on board, regretting he hasn't seen more groups of hammerheads, concludes, as if consoling himself, "Of course, Cocos isn't Disneyland." No. Not yet.

～

> There was a story told before Christ of a fisherman of Boeotia named Glaucus who found an herb to revive fish as they lay gasping on shore. He ate it himself and was changed into a sea thing, half fish half man.
> —Charles Olsen,
> *Call Me Ishmael*

The larger world. Dave's Irish, an accountant working in the Cayman Islands, soon to return to Dublin. Steve's Australian, a pilot based in Hong Kong, on board with Fern, his Thai fiancée. Jorge is Puerto Rican from New York, working in a nuclear power plant. As we finish our last dive, these terrestrial points of origin begin to reassert their significance. Rinsing off my gear for the last time—more water—I have a flash of life on land, think of the hotel in San José, Costa Rica, still thirty-five water hours away, its photo gallery of (only recently) distinguished guests. Henry Kissinger; Warren Beatty; Joe DiMaggio; Napoleon Duarte (President of El Salvador, abetting U.S. mayhem there, no?). Miss Universe 1985. James H. Baker III, famous in his day. In the swim of the human community, all of them.

As we make the long run back to Puntarenas, there are videos on the small screen. Eastwood's *The Unforgiven*. Stallone in *Cliffhanger,* which, given my angle as I doze, reaches me as an intermittent soundtrack. DeVito and Schwarzenneger: *Twins. Wall Street;* Garth Brooks in concert. Videos of our diving. Technology cubed.

Until the films utterly consume us, we have several hours to watch Cocos recede before it's lost in the clouds. Remora-toting bottlenose dolphins again play the bow wave, surfacing to vault or sommersault as we whistle, cheer. In time, however, if ever so slowly, Cocos begins to lose depth, becomes two dimensional. Becomes memory; becomes, inevitably, a function of imagination; becomes syllables.

Ocean: Pre‑ and Post‑Cocos

Before the trip to Cocos, getting in water shape in Hawai'i, aspects of my normal surf routine:

- The recent convert to surfing. "Did you see my ride?" she asks, having caught both a wave and one of surfing's most common viruses.
- Arms exhausted, aching; a day spent trying *not* to go out surfing.
- A memory of the previous late summer, water thick and tepid, as if cooled down from some higher temperature.
- Where do swells go? Was the surf resting last night, did it then get up before us?
- Living near the ocean, one's measured by its terms, the larger society's calibrations less relevant. Unlike, say, a club where the wealthy play golf, where the game's important but still money sets the frame.

By this warm ocean, there's a polyphrenia: regulars on the beach or out at the surf breaks become aware of real-world status—who works as a waiter after surfing, who has nothing but time on his hands; who can or can't afford to live right near the water. Still, here, waves breaking, breaking, here water is a leveler, becomes the unit of measure. Like death, or health, it evens the odds.

❀ Lulls that go on too long should disturb. No waves means, ultimately, no wind. And no wind means, ultimately, no sun.

❀ Waves: varied as snowflakes, they say. Countless molecules in each snowflake, they say.

❀ An enormous south swell, biggest in perhaps twenty years—many waves with two-story faces. Literally hundreds of rescues by lifeguards on jet skis. "How was?" one asks a surfer coming in, knowing the code, that the fellow's obliged to be laconic in the face of an interrogative.

Why this obligation? The cool of restraint, of course. But also, a form of respect for what's beyond words, that can't—or shouldn't—be said. The almost ineffable being … the almost ineffable.

The surfer waits several beats. "Five to seven," he then replies, hyperbole in the service of understatement never an excess.

❀ Surfing as a full-time job: before the Gingrichians subverted the National Endowment for the Arts, I was going to propose fellowships for soul surfers.

❀ Sunset, on-shore wind suddenly down, damped, as if sobered, apologetic for so rudely blowing the waves over.

⚘ Stalking a wave, a surfer misjudges, pulls back, safe but embarrassed: cat that's missed its prey.

⚘ So many tattoos on the beach: shoulder, buttock, small of the back, ankle. Visiting mainland Hell's Angels and lowriders perhaps dismayed by this devaluation of their currency. A passing Samoan, however, with hip-to-knee bodysuit tattoo, the awesome *pe'a*, no doubt unfazed.

⚘ A businessman-neighbor has a big-wave gun shaped for him, costly anticipation outrunning physical capacity. Many surfers are gear freaks, love nuances of board and fin form, but in the water can equipment make the man? No: even in a dollar culture in which appearance is reality, in which simulacra command their own respect, nothing can buy the ability even to get out past the shore break in large surf, much less bestow the courage and skill to ride large waves.

Still, this man's premature purchase of the board may not be all bad. An inducement to the self, promise of commitments to be honored? Or an index of admiration, a yearning to possess the extraordinary grace of fine surfers.

⚘ Sunbathing women, dozing, topless and very well oiled. The waves "collect, overbalance, and fall," Virginia Woolf wrote, until the whole world—even "the heart in the body which lies in the sun on the beach"—seems to be saying "that is all." "Fear no more, says the heart. Committing its burden to some sea, which sighs collectively for all sorrows, and renews, begins, collects, lets fall."

That was England, the Atlantic, the 1920s. Here in the tropics, now, a young woman adjusts the earphones of her Sony Walkman, levitates her upper body to be able to oil herself once again, hands carefully working flesh—thoroughly, as if it is someone else's, someone to whom she should be very attentive—and then turns, falls to the sand with a small groan of pleasure.

- Surfer Mark Foo's death. Foo's body was found. Speaking of the ocean's sodium cycle, Bill Green writes, "The sea keeps nothing, returns all. That is its secret, its identity."

- The thoughtful doctor, man of many commitments—environmental work; social justice—who also surfs and writes poems. Who calls waves "involutions." I look the word up. A state of being involved; complication. A retrograde or degenerative change. A correlative of evolution. The return of an organ to normal size after being distended. A part rolling or curling inward in a spiral, having the whorls wound closely around the axis.

My water involutions: a friend's apartment at the seawall near Diamond Head, just above the surf. Row of palms below his *lānai*—"My babes," he calls them, studying them appreciatively as they sway in the moonlight, their endless hula in the trades. "The mantra of the palms," he terms it. Steve Miller band once again working their magic.

This friend, a Sixties savorer of fine things, loves being out there in the waves, is also a student of the Dow, playing Standard *&* Poor 500 futures with a wry delight in Nuance and Change, betting the economy as a whole an hour or two at a time. He shows me computer printouts charting the curve of a day's trading, explains that "tide watchers" buy and sell stock by anticipating ebbs and flows of price. "Hey," my friend explains, "it's all wave pattern recognition. That and weather forecasting. Same as surfing." My friend clear that surfing of course requires not only physical ability but heightened intuition and, even, spiritual awareness. (Not that one would ever say so.)

Small waves this morning, but glassy. No wind. On the screen of the cerebral cortex clarifies the word, that these sweet vortexes are … Oh, the male gaze. These particular waves evoking the uplifting curve of teeny-bopped & tank-topped breasts. (According to Robert Calasso, Phimedia fell in love with Poseidon, would go to down to the sea, raising the "water from the waves … [to] pour it over her breasts. A gesture of love … motion of feminine substance toward the other … A motion that cannot be satisfied, satisfied only in its unfailing repetition.")

Water, gender: sometimes the ocean is a dominatrix. Shrieking at the (male) surfer, "Get down here." Surfer tied, bound. At other times, water's coy, saying to the surfer courting (her), "Go away, stop paying so much attention." (Surfers for sure paying attention, which must be a form of love.) Waves disappearing to prove the point. Surfers on their bellies, paddling penitents: "Please, baby, please." Or the ocean as crone haunting flea markets, thrift shops: collecting, collecting.

All the young males, waxing their sticks, each sculpted torso with built-in body armor, evoking the *cuirasse esthetique,* schema of muscle architecture used by the ancients to design breastplates. Board—hard; surfer—hard. Surfer after surfer launching, paddling out, leaving shore behind to take on what is in its crazily various aspects both nurturing arena of play and, as they say, raging main. "The inhuman vast," as Dan Duane puts it.

Surfers, familiar phenomenon of fingers wrinkling, skin sagging, water having leeched oil from flesh, skin thus too *dry.* The more important issue for surfers, of course—to avoid getting too wet. (This though for much of Creation life consists of taking in water and reducing its loss, animals being, as Doug Stewart puts it, "a watery solution inside a not-always-watertight bag of skin." When humans lose a tenth of their weight in water, for instance, they become delirious.) *Deliquescence:* to become liquid by attracting or absorbing moisture. Surfers with wrinkled fingers trying—*hard*—not to deliquesce. (But then there's Dionysus. God of the vine, of the juices of life, himself often a liquid as read by Calasso, god of all that is moist, the god who touches the vulva. And Alpheus, who, when his beloved turned to water, agreed to become water himself, "the ultimate erotic convergence.")

Young Greg sits on the beach after a session, having chased away some demons. Often moody. "Had to get to the waves today," he says. "Was drying out." As we sit there, staring at the breaks, surfer up over here, down over there, I ask Greg what gender the ocean is. He laughs: answer's obvious. "Male *and* female," he says. "Or else it wouldn't be there."

～

> I remember what [Linus] Pauling had written about water. I … was utterly taken by the mystery of it: how water retained, like a childhood memory, a trace of its past as ice. How it never forgot that. How it carried that singular fact with it—in its bonds and structures, in its very being—all the way to the boiling point, to where it no longer existed as a liquid. It was water's memory that explained so much, that explained everything, really.
>
> —Bill Green,
> *Water, Ice, and Stone*

Water: so omnipresent one can almost not notice it. Reading water: harder than it looks, if only because all is flux, everything. Consoled by a Seamus Heaney line, which, as he no doubt intended, will take some time to chew on.

> *Air and ocean known as antecedents*
> *Of each other. In apposition with*
> *Omnipresence, equilibrium, brim.*

Something irreducible about both water and strong poetic language, each a kind of prime number ...

Staring at the waves, wondering what to make of them. Not that I'm alone in this. Poet A. R. Ammons: "The very longest swell in the ocean, I suspect, carries the deepest memory." And just what might such waves be like? Some open ocean swells have lengths of nearly half a mile; and of course the tides are themselves huge waves created by the gravitational tug of the sun and moon "while the earth rotates by underneath," as Drew Kampion puts it.

Still, what to make of the waves, after yet another day spent watching, watching. Walking along the seawall near Diamond Head one day with writer Stephen Mitchell, visiting from California, I tell him it had occurred to me while out surfing that death would come as a wave. Not that I would die from a wipeout, but that death would approach as a wave of energy in the form of light. Stephen, who has not only practiced Zen Buddhism but is a reader blessed with great recall, responds that my idea reminds him of something in the work of Buddhist writer Yasutani Roshi. Later, back on the mainland, Stephen cannot locate Yasutani's book, but refers me to Mel Weitsman, who lives in a zendo in Berkeley.

From Mel, I obtain *Eight Beliefs of Buddhism* (1966), in which Hakuun Yasutani elucidates the work of fifth century Indian Seshin Bosatsu. Seshin wrote one thousand books on Buddhism, is called, not surprisingly, Master of One Thousand Books. (Apparently no one chided him for spiritual materialism.) In Seshin's *Yuishiki* (a book Yasutani says takes three years to master), life is compared to a wave. "A wave rises when the energy of the wind passes through the water. That wave, in turn, by its energy, produces the next wave. If there is no resistance or friction this wave action continues endlessly."

Thus, Yasutani reasons, a human's life energy will "produce the next life just as the energy of one wave produces the next wave. This energy will never disappear, resulting in a continuous formation of successive lives. This energy is called 'Karma' ..."

A sweet comparison, though in dispensing with friction Yasutani offers a contrary-to-fact hypothetical. When waves—inevitably—approach shore, "materializing out of the general abstraction of the ocean," as Campion puts it, and "climb into increasing definition," their speed is governed by water depth. As a wave feels the bottom near shore, it slows, adjusts to the contours of the shoaling bottom, and rises in height.

But the issue of friction aside—I have no wish to be ... abrasive—Yasutani reminds us that with waves it is not the water that moves horizontally but energy. Similarly, he argues, there is no fixed "I," no permanent thing such as an ego or soul. Further, Yasutani writes, it may seem that "the moment of death (that is, the end of one swell of the wave) is the end of life and that all energy is lost at the moment of death." But this too is a misapprehension: "Our life is created and destroyed from moment to moment with a new self continually being formed." Our fundamental karma, "the source or the foundation of our personality, has no relation to birth or death." This too may be so, though anyone watching the tremendous energy that bursts out of a wave as it reaches shore—the extraordinary power given via the sun to the wind to the water—anyone watching this inevitably senses *something* being concluded. Expiring.

For Yasutani, a last water comparison: one's Buddha-Nature, the pure or original self, "is like the ocean, and each individual is a wave on the surface of the ocean." I stare at the surfers out in the lineup. It's sunset, and they're beginning to lose definition, their dark shapes now evoking, say, otters as they paddle toward the sweet spot of an incoming wave. But surfers themselves as waves on Buddha-Nature? This I'll have to ponder, especially on days when there are no waves, sky gray, both my senses and the ocean flat—without, as it were, the capacity for metaphor.

(Water and the analogies it inspires. Requires. Peter Ouspensky, a Russian novelist and philosopher born in the late nineteenth century, spent much of his life searching for a higher form of consciousness. Once, aboard ship in a storm in the Sea of Marmora, he felt the "waves were drawing my soul to themselves. And suddenly I felt it went to them. It lasted an instant, perhaps less than an instant, but I entered into the waves and with them rushed with a howl at the ship … the waves, they were myself."

Obsessed with the issue of eternal recurrence, Ouspensky wrote (in *A New Model of the Universe*) that waves—undulatory vibrations—travel in complete circles. Waves also consist of smaller waves and are components of larger waves. "Simply for the sake of argument," Ouspensky suggested, think of days as small

waves forming bigger waves of years which in turn form one great
wave of life … which, he argued, must itself form a curve and
make "a complete revolution, coming back to the point of its departure … the point of death coinciding with the point of birth.")

⌒

I have been shipwrackt, yet am not enemy with the sea.

—Sir Thomas Browne

My surfer's ocean: not just analogies but much play, despite the
risks (many Australian surfers wear helmets, for instance). But returning to California after the Cocos dive trip, I experience weeks
of inadvertent *deep* sleep, even on terra firma continuing to rock
in the swell for days and days. Have trouble losing my sea legs, so
to speak. And, subsequently, I find myself glad to be writing about
water, in my study several miles from San Francisco Bay, several
more miles from the Golden Gate and Pacific.

A neighbor tells me he loves living near the water. And it's
true, the bay affects our climate. Moderates both cold and heat,
creates, with the ocean and the sun, our fogs. And yet, though it's
only a short bike ride, a shorter drive, we're not really close
enough to the ocean to be under its spell—to hear waves break, for
instance—though of course we're nearer to it than are people in
Peoria. To live on water, however, having each day inflected by
water—as when I stay in Hawai'i—is something quite different.

Occasionally, time to go down to the bay to circumnavigate
the former city dump, landfill that's now a shoreline park.
Walking as joggers, in-line skaters, bicyclists, and dogs with or
without owners trot past. The bay, on a windless early winter

morning, like the pool at the foot of a fountain. Too ringed in with city, only the lightest pulse of energy reaching the breakwater.

My respite from water's dynamism, its relentless action, movement. Finally, just before the winter solstice, I head up past Bodega Bay, north of the estuary at Salmon Creek, once more to ocean. I've known this coast's wind and fogs for twenty years, the hard winter rains and long dry summers, spent some of those decades on a ranch just inland, endless days on the veranda studying turkey vultures, cattle, hawks, sheep, cypress, the creek, deer. Now, clambering down the cliff, standing on the shore, expecting the familiar inadvertent rush of pleasure whenever I again see open water, I'm surprised to note that my feelings are mixed: still I'm processing the diving at Cocos. And then it comes to me: this time, the sensation of again reaching the ocean is akin to seeing a former lover. A lover, that is, from a quite intense but often stormy relationship. A lover whom, despite such intimacy, despite so many, many shared pleasures, there's been very good reason to avoid.

Haoles in Paradise

※

The South Pacific islands were held to be the most compatible latitude for Europeans ... to deteriorate physically and spiritually ... struggling against physical and moral decadence, unable to adjust themselves to the alien environment, in spite of its lush tropical beauty.

—W. Somerset Maugham

American missionaries used to complain ... that the problem with Hawaiians was that they lacked sufficient self-contempt. Eating, laughing, and copulating too much, while never working too long, the islanders simply could not understand how rotten they were. The whole Judeo-Christian cosmology ... of a human nature inherently corrupted by sin ... had to be laid on them ... Only then, when they were sufficiently disgusted with themselves, would they be prepared to become like us, 'civilized.'"

—Marshall Sahlins,
"Goodbye to Tristes Tropes"

Throughout the island world of the Pacific, scattered men of many European races and from almost every grade of society carry activity and disseminate disease. Some prosper, some vegetate.

—Robert Louis Stevenson,
The Ebb-Tide

Stevenson, of course, was writing at the end of the nineteenth century. Fifty years later, thousands of American military personnel passed through Hawai'i en route to the Pacific front. Postwar films and TV shows such as "Hawaii Five-O" continued to present a version of Hawai'i and the Pacific as—even with crimes to be solved—paradise, and mass air travel made Hawai'i vacations for the middle and lower middle class possible. Some vacationers, like some military retirees after the war, stayed on. At Waikīkī and down toward Diamond Head, you see the postwar shoreline buildings, five- to ten-story condos: Pacific Sands, Tropic Shores, that kind of thing. Native Hawaiians and other "locals" (people of color, the term meant, as opposed to local or mainland *haoles*—whites) tended not to buy into these buildings. Often they had large families; the apartments were too small or expensive. The Elks Club and Outrigger Canoe Club were down here; retirees and childless couples who bought condos had a social life set for them if they chose. Ocean in front, Diamond Head behind, Kapi'olani Park right there. Amazing, really: paradise. All this and a few Hawaiian words in one's vocabulary—*aloha, mahalo, mauka, maka'i, pau hana.*

The house rules of many of these buildings were written in the Fifties, reflecting laws and attitutes then current. And, often, board members running these buildings failed to keep up with changes in the law. It was not surprising, then, that even in the late Eighties some owners' associations had committees interviewing prospective buyers, as if—twenty years after the Civil Rights Movement and after Affirmative Action and Equal Opportunity—they could prevent someone 'undesirable' from moving in without the threat of litigation. Some associations also had house rules governing occupancy (in effect, no extended families) and precluding children except as short-term visitors—grandkids at Christmas and in summer was the ideal. Thus the buildings had a visible absence both of the young and, because of the small apartments and steep prices, of adults of child-bearing and child-rearing age. Finally, the elected boards running these buildings were often comprised of the first generation of owners, and were administered by resident concierges who'd been in their jobs for years, were confidants of, or dependent on, that first set of owners. The geriatric quality of political power in the buildings was best evidenced at annual meetings, when one could see who actually ran the place, push come to shove. In some of these cooperatives, there was a kind of Oedipal revolt waiting to be expressed.

A decade or so ago, a couple in their thirties who'd lived in one of these buildings for years had a child. These were water people— loved their small apartment close to the ocean. They moved out when the baby was born, but then moved back in, in effect challenging the house rule. While agreeing they'd signed the purchase agreement, they argued Federal law had changed. How could they be asked to honor an illegal discriminatory restriction? Some owners were incensed: a deal was a deal; they didn't want kids living in the building; three people in a studio (with enclosed *lānai*) violated the occupancy density rule; the building wasn't safe for kids (though kids were present as visitors) … these were among their arguments. Finally, the board served the couple with an eviction notice.

The ensuing legal struggle lasted five years. The law's an odd thing—not only slow, but right and wrong are often not the issue. What may appear discriminatory may not be; what may appear to have been an agreement may not be. Meanwhile, lawyers have their own priorities, and, it must be recalled, get paid by the hour or fraction thereof. May or may not have a stake in ending litigation, however high-minded or unpleasant the client. May or may not themselves be competent. Prima facie, to use a legal Latinism, how might a client be sure?

Litigants, meanwhile, often begin by demanding from the legal process what it seldom provides: vindication, justice, true compensation. And then you have the insurance companies: the buildings carry insurance—a possible pot of gold—so the strategies and lawyers of the companies providing it also become variables, players. Add to this that any trial of this issue in Hawai'i might, finally, play out before a jury of "locals," whereas both the couple and the board members would be read as *"haoles."* A jury might be pro-family, but also might see all the litigants as well-off and as outsiders (even if here for decades), whatever the merits of the case. Which might affect an award of damages, if any. That is, you could win and still have lost thousands of dollars in legal fees.

Through all of this, the couple continued to live in their apartment. As before their child was born, they swam, kayaked, surfed, boogie-boarded, walked the seawall, watched sunset and long afterglow, ignited fireworks on the Fourth of July. Almost no one in the area spent more time in and by the water, made it more central to their lives. But now the couple had to contend with the bitterness of many of their co-owners, as well as installments on lawyer's bills and endless hours discussing strategy. Even initial victories in the legal process, it turned out, meant only more litigation, years of it probably. Meant more and more time telling their story, explaining, justifying.

Some of the couple's fellow owners, meanwhile—including people with whom they'd once shared the joy of this beautiful, endlessly shape-changing, warm ocean—pressed for legal annihilation of the couple, would appeal to the Supreme Court if necessary, volunteered to subsidize the fight out of their own pockets. Other owners tried to propose a way out of the madness of litigation—there was from traditional Hawaiian culture a still-used process of mediation called *ho'oponopono*— but to no avail.

Pono, righteousness, goodness, as in the state motto: *Ua mau ke ea o ka 'āina e ka pono*—forever the life of the land in righteousness. But in Hawai'i, with the karma of land since the erosion and overthrow of the kingdom by Americans in the nineteenth century, and given the role of Western concepts of private property in this unrelenting dispossession of the Hawaiian *maka'āinana*—common people—from the land—*'āina*—of which some argue the chiefs served as stewards, not owners … Given all this, just where might righteousness, *pono,* be located in a quarrel about real estate? What kind of process of restitution might it take? How many wrongs would be righted? A terrible burden, for sure, far too much for any individual. But still, there it was, something that willy-nilly accompanied title to the land. Nothing simple about "fee simple."

It's weird, unfair. Times don't just change: paradigms shift. Suddenly, what everyone just a moment ago seemed collectively to hold to be true is … different, altered, gone. Native Hawaiians dispossessed, marginalized; winning the war after Pearl Harbor; statehood, ending territorial status, that great civic imperative; the rise to power of Asian-Americans: all of this achieved, achieved. But now, as if in a dream, history was being redefined. Old sins, omissions, ghosts, seeking correction, justice. *Pono.* Now families with children would have larger rights? Ah, well and good. But who else, then? On what past was the whole edifice resting? Who would help, who would hinder, who would just stand by? Who would do something, anything, not simply in his or her own direct self-interest?

Meanwhile, normal urban life went on—Honolulu is a city, after all. A murder. A robbery. A domestic dispute. Noise from the building next door. Hassles with parking. There were also arguments about how much renovation the building required, some owners less than eager to spend to protect the future. And yet another renter who'd tried Hawai'i for a few years moved back to the "mainland." Too far from kids and friends, a sense of being out of place. A *haole* where the term seemed ever more pejorative, especially given the commemoration of the one hundredth anniversary of the overthrow of Queen Lili'uokalani by American businessmen and Marines.

Oh, some people in the building might have said if polled, "Come on, the Hawaiian monarchy was corrupt. The chiefs sold the commoners out. And anyway, there were different waves of Native immigration to Hawai'i: these Hawaiians enslaved Polynesians who came before them. Not to mention the late eighteenth century, after whites arrived, when Kamehameha "unified" the islands with his battles. And then there was human sacrifice and the restrictions on women. And the kingdom would have been overthrown anyway by Germany or Japan or Britain. Its time had come." You could say all this, believe it, but still the moral ground was shifting.

As for the lawsuit: in the end, not surprisingly, a deal was cut. It cost the insurance company, though they'd no doubt survive;

and cost the building and thus each of the apartment owners something, but not more than they could afford. As for the couple, they received a chunk of money and some changes in the house rules—a form of apology, surely—though whether living on the ocean during those years of litigation was worth the downside risk and bad feeling, who can tell? What would be the arithmetic? Perhaps, savoring yet another miraculous south swell, at high tide riding the backwash from the seawall, shot out and up and over still one more incoming wave, perhaps the insanity was for the couple cleansed by water. Abluted. Perhaps so. What does seem certain, in any case, is that for some time to live in this building in Honolulu was not at all to live in paradise.

The Literary Pacific

Native and Stranger, capitalised, may seem a little romantic and ab‹
stract. They are not meant to be, and they are not. Polynesian Native
and European Stranger initial encounters were violent ... The Poly‹
nesian words that describe this opposition of Native and Stranger are
certainly not romantic: _kamdaina/haole_ in Hawaii, _maohi/papaa_ in
Tahiti, _enata/aoe_ in the Marquesas, _tagata/paplangi_ in Samoa,
maori/pakeha in New Zealand.

> —Greg Dening,
> _Islands and Beaches_

Fa fisi: from the Rotuman—white man.

I seem always to have been a reader. Third of four children of two
very literate parents, I was early on scarfing up the books of my
older siblings, both savoring and sparring with words in a house-
hold in which language was art, shield, music, weapon. As for the
Pacific, in the Boston of my childhood—Nahant, Crane's Beach,
Bar Harbor, and Nantucket our family's most freqent saltwater
destinations—it was Heyerdahl's raft in _Kon Tiki_, Nordhoff and

Hall's *Mutiny on the Bounty,* and *Robinson Crusoe* that initially registered most strongly. By the time I got to college, Joseph Conrad's Pacific had absorbed me, and, of course, Herman Melville's. I did not fail to note, for instance, that the *Pequod*'s voyage in *Moby Dick* begins in New Bedford and Nantucket: terra cognita.

Black sheep of this book-absorbed family (our mother a very accomplished poet) I rebelled by … setting out to write. Still, to try this outside of academia was somehow not to be done, at least for the male children, if only given reasonable parental cautions about needless jeopardy. Thus, I was able both to emulate authors I'd read and to feel like James Dean as I did so. A marvelous explosive mix, particularly given the context of the mid- and late Sixties, but also a way of reconciling Dionysian excess with the world of my childhood—by telling stories.

In my twenties, when I had still simply published one book, when there were many other things to do, many other things I could or might do, long before I realized the depth of my commitment to, need of, writing, I began to spend time in the tropics, initially in the then-funky outer islands of Hawai'i. It surprised me not at all that I was a frequent visitor to the local public library: books were my habit, and I wanted to extend my knowledge with reading about the Pacific, but also to shed light on what might become of me if I stayed too long. Beachcomber? Old Pacific hand? Outcast of the islands? I read fiction, history, anthropology, oceanography.

By the time I came to teach at the University of Hawai'i years later, now an author who'd published a number of books, I was discovering the indigenous postcolonial English-language writers of the Pacific, found them with a writer's excitement at discovering a new body of work. (O explorers, O conquerers!) Until recently, this literature was quite unavailable in the United States; and then I had the good fortune to spend time in the South Pacific to meet some of these writers. Yet another voyage of discovery, possession; of self-discovery, being possessed … Where, then, to begin a tale of my dialogue with these books and writers?

In the early Seventies, as Pacific island nations emerged from colonial domination, an indigenous literature launched itself with clear intent. Vincent Eri's *The Crocodile*, the first Papua New Guinean novel, was published, followed by Maori Witi Ihimaera's *Pounamu* and Samoan Albert Wendt's *Sons for the Return Home*. In Fiji, meanwhile, Cook Islander Marjorie Tuainekore Crocrombe (who'd been a student in Ulli Beier's pioneering writing classes at the recently formed University of Papua New Guinea) and others, especially Albert Wendt, sought to encourage a new literature both by publishing a literary journal, *Mana,* and by offering creative writing classes at the University of the South Pacific in Suva, Fiji (then a new regional university).

In 1978, Alan Barker, an expatriate lecturing at USP, argued in *Mana* that "young and tender" Third World education systems needed to prevent the "death of creative imagination," citing courses that "purport to teach creative writing" as examples of the "suicidal obsession with technological mind." And, "What is perhaps most dangerous in the self-consciousness of this attempt to 'create' a culture is that it prevents the emergence of art with true and honest inspiration; for a true culture … cannot be 'produced.' It is a growth, an organic flowering, an apotheosis."

Responding in less florid prose, Marjorie Crocrombe wrote, "We islanders must do our own writing about our own societies, our own experiences, our own perceptions of the world." And, Albert Wendt argued, "A literature is both a mirror and a map of the mind and soul ... And because we need to know about where we are living now, every culture needs such a map. It is a necessity for the survival of any people. And it has to be their literature. (This does not mean the exclusion of the literature of other peoples.)"

Books Alan Barker might have deemed organic growth could be found in the reading matter "hermit" Tom Neale took to his desert island in the Cooks in 1952: Frisbie, Stevenson, Defoe, Maugham, Nordhoff and Hall, Conrad. All outsiders to the Pacific, some committed to the region, Defoe utterly imagining it, each book part of a two-hundred-year written conversation by the West. And what an envisioning and scrutiny it had been! Think of Malinowski's journals, too-human private subtext to the sophisticated voice of his anthropology; or young Margaret Mead in Samoa for eight months, hurrying toward professional success; or Crusoe's mini-kingdom; or Gaugin's tropical efflorescence (as Gavan Daws put it, "... beached in the Marquesas, with a bad heart and failing eyes, very likely morphine-addicted, possibly leprous, certainly syphilitic.")

In the two-century flow of this rich and strange commentary from without—factor in titles like *The Demystification of Yap,* or *Clio in Oceania*—one encounters books that particularly move or impress: the nineteenth-century memoir of beachcomber William Diapea (*Cannibal Jack, The True Account of a White Man in the South Seas*). Fiji mill overseer Walter Gill's unvarnished, bluntly insightful *Turn Left at the Graveyard.* Totaram Sanadhya's *My Twenty-One Years in the Fiji Islands,* from the Hindi account of his life as an indentured laborer and organizer against the indenture system. *Islands and Beaches,* Australian historian Greg Dening's obsessive, brilliant meditation on the dark fate of the Marquesas. William Bradford Huie's *The Revolt of Mamie Stover,* saga of a entrepreneurial prostitute and social change in World War II Hawai'i. Or Joana McIntyre Varawa's oddly moving search for a lover—and for love—in contemporary Fiji in *Changes in Latitude.* Books larger and smaller, but each with the authority of hard-earned experience and insight.

We also sense, however, and in historian Dening's work are made explicitly aware of, what is absent in this literature: stories told by the indigenous peoples; their version. Given our recognition of the negative space in even these compelling narratives, it's no surprise to also encounter books in which the hazards of writing from the outside become cautionary exemplums. Where words, if inadvertently, do violence to the truth. Take archeologist/anthropologist Robert Suggs's *Marquesan Sexual Behavior,* published in the late Fifties. Here the *mana* brought home to the United States will be slightly prurient "data" delivered in social-scientific deadpan, the academic mask of the time. For instance, Suggs writes that males often conducted "comparative sessions at which the length of the penis is measured along the extended palm and arm, in the Marquesan fashion of indicating lengths." Talk about participant-observation: Suggs says he was often asked for his tape measure! Or, raising the question of bestiality, then obligatory in inventories of sexual proclivity, Suggs writes that "A very frequently overheard reference was that to copulation with chickens. It was stated, most commonly, that in intercourse the chicken would gyrate wildly, flapping its wings, producing a cooling breeze. This was called the 'Nuku Hiva fan' by informants."

Overheard. It was stated. Informants. Other outsider pratfalls in the Pacific have been more mean spirited. Think of James Michener, who in the Fifties found Fiji a "really wonderful colony": "It is almost impossible to like the Indians of Fiji. They are suspicious, vengeful, whining, unassimilated, provocative aliens in a land where they have lived for more than seventy years. They hate everyone: black natives, white Englishmen, brown Polynesians, and friendly Americans."

Not only had Michener apparently not read or met activist Totararm Sanadhya, but his willingness to caricaturize suggests he'll never be accountable to the people about whom he writes. Never, that is, exposed to *their* story about him. Another peril of outsider literature, however, is that in it one can hear a counterstory. Marquesan laughter, for instance, behind the "data" Suggs records—could he really have believed the chicken story; is he putting his sponsors on?—and the sense that Suggs's books are rivaled by a Marquesan version of his stay. Could Margaret Mead have failed to understand she was being teased, not realized her endless questions provoked ever more hyperbolic response? (Or, if she believed her informants or translator, surely she sensed she was pushing their stories to conclusions they could not carry.) And, even as recent Pacific traveler Paul Theroux wins another argument he records—what a wheel of recurrence!—he evokes that stock character of Hawai'i, the truculent mainland *haole*. (For a parody of this familiar type, listen to the late Rap Reiplinger's "Room Service" on the album *Poi Dog*.)

Given the hazards of outsider literature, it is Greg Dening's brooding response that seems most determinedly human. About doing historical research in the Marquesas, Dening writes:

> I discovered my limitations in language and knowledge and wished that
> I might stay to plumb the silence of the Land a little deeper. For I should

have known that the dead are easier to talk to than the living. I should have known the cost of hearing somebody through the silence. On the beach one is so deaf to words, so blind to gestures: on the beach one knows oneself in caricature because of the differences, but others hardly at all. That is my regret, then, that I do not know the living Men as I know the dead; and I have this half-suspicion that Aoe [Outsiders, Strangers] bring their silence with them.

Finally, as the reader may by now have gathered, there's one other risk for whites in the tropics in the late twentieth century. This being a variant of the notorious nineteenth-century "Polynesian paralysis," a kind of dengue fever of the soul. Which is, the impulse to establish oneself as special outsider. The "good *haole* complex," we might term it. Tropics awash in revisionist history, "and revolution in the air" as Bob Dylan once put it—not to mention the sound of tumbrils—any outsider is confronted with his position vis-à-vis both that history and outsiders ignorant or in denial of it. There is, almost inevitably, a revulsion of the hordes of similar-seeming others. Comes then the too-human hunger to set oneself apart, to sacrifice these others if necessary (more [*haole*]cannibalism!).

"Hawai'i's a totally appropriated place," an insightful visiting academic in Hawai'i tells me, including herself in the indictment. A Ph.D. made her sophisticated in reading dynamics of gender, race, class. She does not, however, feel that Boston, where she's from, is "totally appropriated." Of course she knows the history of Puritan New England, the massacre and displacement of Native Americans, but nonetheless, Boston's her turf. An achiever in the middle class, in Boston she is also, as they used to say, hip—crosses all kinds of class and ethnic boundaries.

But in the Islands? Possessor of a visitor's plum in the imperium's educational system, albeit as subversive? The effect of such felt anomalies leads her to conclude she's doing *less* appropriating than other non-Natives. She explicates the subtle interactions of capitalism/imperialism/colonialism/sexism; uses the word *privilege* as both verb and noun; works, hard, to mentor local students. Goes to Kapi'olani Park to hear Israel Kamakawiwo'ole, dazzled by the vast corpulence that contains, from which emerges ... pure voice, pure heart. Is moved, her own heart full of *aloha* for everyone around her. In subsequent weeks, glow of the concert fading, still she knows she has a special connection to the Islands. Thus, despite ambivalences about her place in Hawai'i even as a visitor, she does not give up her position (though who would ask her to—life's complex; the Good takes many forms).

Like some of her new colleagues, this visitor declares her affiliation with one of the Hawaiian groups. But how does an outsider read the Other so quickly; how can even a sophisticated student of theory choose among the many bitterly opposed Native factions? The risk is a kind of narcissism, support for leaders well educated in Western terms, who speak fluently to the (*haole*) media, who are like ... like one would herself be, were she Native Hawaiian. Such leaders, however, are sometimes termed "*haole-fied*" by other Natives, who are in return deemed "colonized." You see the quandary ...

Or, a related hazard: how avoid attributing moral superiority to any particular descendent of victims of historical wrong? How bear in mind that innate virtue may manifest itself no more frequently in the oppressed than in the oppressor? How insist that to argue what the past might *otherwise* have been is a kind of quicksand? As one resident of Hawai'i, speaking of this visiting academic with both sympathy and fatigue, puts it, "She wants to be forgiven for things she didn't do. But also to blame others more than herself." So far, there seems no innoculation against such powerful viruses.

Once, just back on the mainland from a four-month stay in the Pacific, I went with a Chinese-American friend to a local sushi restaurant. Japanese-born chef a reggae lover. Bob Marley on the boom box. Several of the males at the counter were that peculiar mutant, the California neo-redneck playing loveably hip lout: gourmet tastes *cum* pickup. Lots of facial hair. Voices too loud. Taking this all in, no doubt suffering from a kind of Stockholm syndrome, identifying with my captors—the Pacific Islanders I'd recently spent so much time around—I stage whispered to my friend, only half-kidding, "Jesus Christ, so many fuckin' *haoles*."

⟨~⟩

Suggested over-the-counter medication for the good *haole* syndrome (no prescription needed, but no liability assumed). Consider the enthymeme, a syllogism in which one premise is unexpressed. A proposition in which one of the arguments is not stated. Which, if explicit, may render the argument more complex—or less suasive. For instance: *I love you.* That chameleon phrase. At a given moment of stress between anxious mates, the whole thought may in fact read: 1) I love you. 2) Love is good and should be reciprocated. 3) Therefore, you should love me. As with love, so with the past: what to do about it now, where one stands, who has what authority to speak, who owes what to whom and why. That is, one must hear the argument spelled out, whatever the heart is saying.

⟨~⟩

Both sides of the story. In the social sciences, there's been a recent revisionist effort to reimagine the initial encounters of outsiders and Pacific Islanders. Sahlins, Dening, Obeyesekere, Kame'elei-hiwa, and others have done much to insist that of course there were stories, myth-making, and interpretations on both sides. (In *The Apotheosis of Captain Cook,* for instance, native Sri Lankan Gananath Obeyesekere argues that it was not the Hawaiians but the English who had the need to make Cook a god.) Remarkably, Connolly and Anderson's *First Contact* gives the commentary of the still-living. In 1930, exploring the interior of Papua New Guinea, then presumed by the Australian colonial administration to be uninhabited, prospector Michael Leahy was astonished to encounter natives: "... presently the camp was swarming with the lot of them, all running about and jabbering at once ..."

Jabbering, yes, in one of the many—eight hundred, they say— languages of the Papuan highlands. As Steven Pinker points out, "No mute tribe has ever been discovered ... The universality of complex language is a discovery that fills linguists with awe ... There are Stone Age societies, but there is no such thing as a Stone Age language."

As Pinker explains, during Leahy's exploration of the high-lands the natives' scrutiny of his group was overwhelming, hun-dreds of people at a time "gazing at us like prize cattle at a country show." Natives not just looking: seeing white men for the first time, one highlander said, "the people sat down and developed stories." And investigated. For instance, trying to ascertain whether or not these strangers were spirits, one highlander apparently hid to watch them defecate. "He came back and said, 'Those men from heaven went to excrete over there.' Once they had left many men went to take a look. When they saw that it smelt bad, they said, 'Their skin might be different, but their shit smells bad like ours.'" Or so the highlander's story goes ...

Though a writer, I have no impulse to elevate written language above dance, music, surfing, or song. The world's full of miracles, many of which I for one cannot begin to apprehend. But if we are to speak of writing, the Barker debate of the late Seventies notwithstanding, there was of course already literature by indigenous Pacific Islanders. In Hawai'i alone there were Hawaiian-language newspapers through much of the nineteenth century, and Pi'ilani's memoir of her wilderness years with her husband Ko'olau, published in 1906.

By the time Pi'ilani was born, some one hundred years after Cook arrived in Hawai'i, there were perhaps fifty thousand Native Hawaiians, down from a population (revisionist) historian David Stannard argues may have been five hundred thousand or more. There was also, by 1870, leprosy, one of the many new imports from the outer world. In 1865, the Hawaiian kingdom began transporting the afflicted to a remote peninsula on the island of Moloka'i. In 1893, American businessmen and their forces overthrew Queen Lili'uokalani. This so-called Provisional Government sought and finally achieved annexation by the United States.

This, then, is the context of the life and death of the cowboy Kalua-i-Ko'olau. In that momentous year of 1893, at Kalalau Valley on the island of Kaua'i, Ko'olau shot and killed the *haole* sheriff, Louis Stolz, who sought to transport him to Moloka'i without his wife and child. (Or perhaps Ko'olau's wife Pi'ilani shot Stolz: she too was expert with a rifle.) Ko'olau and/or Pi'ilani then shot and killed two of a party of eighty P. G. [Provisional Government] (*haole*) soldiers who came after them, soon after disappearing into the wilderness with their son.

In 1907, American writer Jack London reached Hawai'i. After a nightmare voyage on the expensive yacht he'd had built, socialist

London sympathized with Native Hawaiians, but also now had a valet in his entourage, and nagging large debts. While traveling, London wrote every day, much of his labor piece work for magazines. One of the crew on London's voyage was Bert Stolz, a Stanford University student raised on Kaua'i, son of Louis Stolz, the sheriff killed by Ko'olau. Not surprisingly, what London heard from Bert Stolz became grist for the writer's mill: "Koolau the Leper" appeared in 1912. About this story, the late A. Grove Day noted, "… it is fiction, not fact," which Day attributes to "the needs of fiction." One sees, however, that London's Ko'olau was instantly familiar to London's readers: a defiant hero with a just cause. In his telling, London increased the number of deaths, made vengeance by Ko'olau a theme, had Ko'olau betrayed by his own people, and included a gallant *haole* army captain, obligatory because of London's belief in the superiority of whites.

The year before London's voyage to Hawai'i, however, Pi'ilani (who, like her son, fails to appear in London's saga) published her own story. If London was writing in English to readers of popular magazines, Pi'ilani, writing in Hawaiian with the help of John Sheldon (Kahikina Kelekona), had a different audience in mind: "My companions of this same race with whom I talk of this true story I am stringing as a garland of remembrance for my husband and our budding beloved child, if perhaps you were with me at this time …, perhaps you would not lack for sympathy …" And, Pi'ilani writes, "While my husband was speaking to our friends, I wept, and if you had been there with me, my readers, you would also have wept for the sadness." (Translation by Frances Frazier.)

As it turns out, the three of them never left the Kalalau Valley. After nearly two years, their son died of leprosy. Worse, Pi'ilani could see her husband begin to fail. A year later, he too died. After some months alone, Pi'ilani returned to the human community.

In 1916, Christopher Blom Hofgaard presented a paper to the Kaua'i Historical Society. Born in Norway, Hofgaard was a merchant on Kaua'i, admired Pi'ilani, wanted "to get from her the story of Ko'olau and his doings ..." But "to get her to talk about her husband ... was often difficult. She ... acted always as if she had a secret fear of being called to answer for her actions in staying by her husband and assisting him in his outlaw life."

Despite Hofgaard's praise for Pi'ilani's physical courage and loyalty to her husband, he was peevish about Pi'ilani's book: "[It] is written in flowing Hawaiian and is difficult to read and translate, as [Sheldon] uses the greatest possible amount of crooked words to record the simplest historical point ..."

Crooked words? Of the soldiers who came after them and burned the homes of their friends, Pi'ilani wrote: "... my husband and I were filled with rage, and if perhaps we could have gotten some of them we would have wrung their bones and fed them to the fire. Until this day I am not done brooding over these plundering, burning, thieving P. G. *kolea*, the birds who come to fatten on our land, who came as wanderers and arrogantly live on the sweet breast of our native land ... my mind is made up never to forget or forgive for the rest of my life."

"Difficult to read and translate," Hofgaard also said of Pi'ilani's book. But Pi'ilani wrote that she wanted to "stand without doubt and fearlessly before my own people of my own race and indeed before the whole world, and tell the true story and only the truth, from beginning to end, of everything concerning the deeds of my beloved husband ..."

At the conclusion of her narrative, Pi'ilani thanked Sheldon, "so accomplished with the pen, for inspiring, arranging, weaving together, and editing this story ... And I affirm to the world that this is the correct, true, and one and only story of Kalua-i-Ko'olau from beginning to end." Before Pi'ilani's book, there had been accounts in both Hawaiian-language and English-language newspapers in Hawai'i. And subsequent to both Pi'ilani's book and the Jack London story, there have been many other lenses. (In Texeira's *Koolau, Leper King of Kalalau Ke Ana,* Sheriff Stolz makes sexual advances to Pi'ilani. And Janion, in "The Leper of Kalalau," reads Stolz as too zealously doing his duty, but has Stolz refer to Ko'olau as his friend. There were of course also written field reports in 1893 from the P. G. commander who led the pursuit of Ko'olau.) Thus, though long since not at all the "one and only story of Kalua-i-Ko'olau ...," Pi'ilani's telling is, surely, the only one with this particular impulse: "I humbly pray that this book will be a memorial for Kalua-i-Ko'olau, that we may all forever keep our love for him and our child unforgotten in our hearts. They sleep in the bosom of Kalalau but will live again in our living memories."

⌒

A note on language. Much of the writing in the contemporary Pacific is in English, a first language for some Pacific Islanders, second for many others, the language of higher education for nearly all. There are also writers, like Joseph Veramu in Fiji, creating fiction in two languages. Though long since we know that the empire does write back, can brilliantly appropriate English, it's also true that native tongues may demand to be restored. Think of Hawai'i, where several years after the overthrow of the kingdom in 1893, the use of Hawaiian in schools was made illegal. Kill a language, the reasoning seemed to go, kill a culture.

Though for many Pacific Island writers English is the language of literacy, the language of the larger audience, or simply the language in which a book made itself available to the author, and despite the genius of, say, Chinua Achebe, Salman Rushdie, Jamaica Kincaid, *et al.*, it may come down to hard choice. For instance, pursuing mastery of written story in English, Epeli Hau'ofa has argued, carried the cost of giving up a portion of the mastery he might have achieved in oral story in Tongan. And the sense does recur that of course there are things that just cannot be expressed in a given tongue, or in a tongue not originally of a place, or, can only be expressed in one's mother tongue. (One thinks of analyst Adam Phillips on the acquisition of language—both "innate gift and an imposition on the child … the child may be inventive within it, but it is not the child's invention.")

Scale. Some two hundred sixty million people in the United States, eighteen million in Australia, three million five hundred thousand in New Zealand/Aoteoroa. Five hundred thousand in Fiji, one hundred seventy thousand in Western Samoa (another thirty-five thousand in American Samoa, and some one hundred thousand ethnic Samoans in New Zealand, Australia, Hawai'i, California, and Utah). One hundred thousand in Tonga. Thirty thousand in the Cook Islands. Two thousand five hundred on Rotuma. Epeli Hau'ofa has argued, compellingly, against social scientists who, in a perhaps unintentional neoimperialism, read Pacific Islands as "pitiful microstates condemned forever to depend on migration, remittance, aid, and bureaucracy …" In Hau'ofa's "New Oceania," the entire Pacific is the Islanders' home; they inhabit a "sea of islands," are "ocean people" with a heroic history of great voyaging and interconnectedness: "We are the sea, we are the ocean, we must wake up to this ancient truth and together use it to overturn all hegemonic views that aim ultimately to confine us again, physically and psychologically, in the tiny spaces … from which we have recently liberated ourselves."

Economics and/or metaphors aside, however, it's no surprise that, given the size and populations of these islands, there are, as a Samoan warned me, "no secrets." Further, in the Pacific, author and book are seldom divorced from each other. This though the readership of English-language literature on many Pacific islands is limited, though books are enormously expensive, and though for many islanders English is at most a second language. Nonetheless, the author is visible, local, and quite obviously connected to the text. As Hau'ofa says, "In our small Pacific communities the struggle for certain kinds of freedom comes right down to the most personal and intimate levels. It is therefore very difficult, for one is bound to lose the affection of relatives and friends. The feeling of isolation can be acute but is the price one pays for freedom."

If authors are accountable for what they write, on the other hand in the Pacific that same author you dislike inevitably happens also to be your in-law or cousin, or your close friend's in-law or cousin. Someone you know you will continue to (have to) see for years to come. And vice versa. This also means that if you want to write about people it will be hard to disguise them, even in fiction. (In *Mutant Message,* a recent international best-seller about a "summoned" American woman's walkabout—"READ ABOUT INDIGENOUS PEOPLE LIVING THEIR ANCIENT CULTURE"— marketed first as nonfiction and then as fiction, we learn that Australian aborigines are clairvoyant and telepathic because they don't lie. Sobering, something to ponder, though on reflection we can venture that lying must have some redeeming function, if only the miraculous running room of fiction.)

Scale and the role of the writer. A few years ago, I was in a restaurant in Honolulu with a Pacific Island friend when a local journalist walked in. We'd both met her before, nodded as she passed. Hawai'i, with a population of one and a half million, just isn't that big a place. After the journalist was out of earshot, I told my friend that a recent review this woman had written was far too careful to avoid controversy. Hearing this, my friend looked at me as if wondering how even a mainland *haole* could so miss the point. "You know," she said, "she has to live here."

Scale and the Pacifc author as public figure ... Such familiarity can breed if not contempt then underestimation. Recently, in Apia, I met a very well-educated Samoan woman who, improbably, professed never to have gotten through more than a page of any novel by Samoan Albert Wendt. Whether or not she had in fact read Wendt, however, it was no surprise that she'd have an opinion.

Gone Troppo. In 1992, an expatriate professor in Fiji enjoyed arguing that there's no such thing as Pacific literature. This was someone in a state of denial, or, perhaps, envy. But now that an extensive Pacific literature has emerged, what might either side of the Barker debate make of it? In that *Mana* article back in 1978, Barker, no minimalist, wrote: "Art is the emergence of Being out of its concealment, form out of chaos, and it must have that justifying spark which makes the work a living flame beyond any analytical measurement ... it is the essence; the ungraspable."

Justifying spark. The ungraspable. Here, for any reader, is the

issue of the recalcitrance of literature. Or, of writers, their in-
tractability, as well as the (often miraculous) unpredictability of
fiction. How silences end. If Albert Wendt's enormous, brooding
achievement in *Leaves of the Banyan Tree* shocked some Samoan
readers, exposed "family" secrets, think of the work of Tongan Epeli Hau'ofa. That is, when you dream of a literature, could you
have imagined Hau'ofa's second book? Many readers liked the
sweet irreverence and, even, blasphemy, of his earlier *Tales of the
Tikong.* But I learned, encountering the extraordinary *Kisses in the
Nederends,* that many Pacific Islanders—and many outsiders familiar with the Pacific—found it in bad taste. ("Raw, not cooked,"
as Hau'ofa once put it.)

The comedic quest saga of a Pacific Islander who wakes one
morning with a pain in his "Nederends" and his trials with both
Native and Western healers, the novel has a clear impulse—to
mock foible and pretense. Equally clear, however, is that *Kisses* ar-
ticulates serious yearning for a different kind of human community. In a particularly brilliant sequence—the protagonist's dam-
aged fundament is replaced by a transplant from a deceased white
woman—the novel even suggests the possibility of some kind of
inclusive, multiracial, polygendered Pacific communion.

Tongans and writing. In 1806, English seaman William Mariner, then fourteen, a castaway in Tonga, became the king's adopted
son. In the account of his stay elicited by John Martin after
Mariner's return to England, King Finow (Finau 'Ulakalala II) was
puzzled when he first saw writing. "Studying the letters that
spelled his name, he said, 'This is neither like myself, nor anybody
else! Where are my legs? How do you know it to be I?'" The king,
Mariner testified, was particularly impressed by the virtue writing

seemed to possess for love notes, "that he should like to know it himself, and for all the women to know it, that he might make love with less risk of discovery, and not so much chance of incurring the vengeance of their husbands."

Nearly two centuries later, so pragmatic a vision of writing's possibilities might bring a smile to the lips of author Epeli Hauʻofa. Born in 1939 in Papua New Guinea, where his Tongan parents were missionaries, Hauʻofa's initial languages were several Papua New Guinean dialects, his later languages English and Tongan. After some years in Tonga, secondary school in Fiji, and higher education in Canada and Australia, Hauʻofa received a Ph.D. in anthropology (by now he knew yet another Papua New Guinean dialect, as well as Fijian).

By 1975, however, in his mid-thirties, Hauʻofa was finding fault with anthropology: "… pictures of people who fight, compete, trade, pay bride-prices, engage in rituals, invent cargo cults, copulate, and sorcerise each other. There is hardly anything … to indicate whether these people have any such sentiments as love, kindness, consideration, altruism, and so on …" But it was not only the politics of his discipline that alienated Hauʻofa: "I was repelled by the jargon-laden obscurantism, the crassness and crudity of much of the social scientific literature."

In the mid-Seventies, Hauʻofa returned to Tonga as a research fellow and freelance social critic, later becoming a civil servant. In this period, Hauʻofa writes, any Pacific Islander with a higher degree could "literally become whatever he wished to be, or he could become what he had never imagined becoming. In the name of localisation and regionalisation, greatness was liberally showered on unsuspecting persons by the promoters of native peoples." Which

might have been fine, but Hauʻofa was made Deputy Private
Secretary to His Majesty the King of Tonga, only to conclude that
doing so went against the larger half of his nature. A self-described
skeptic, clown, outsider, "and connoisseur of absurdity," an agnos-
tic where participation in church activities was part of one's social
standing, Hauʻofa then turned to the University of the South
Pacific in Fiji. And he continued writing fiction, an extension of
his ethnographic studies, entitled in it to "invent and embellish
freely, entertain, scold, and swear to my heart's content …"

In that earlier time of his return to Tonga, however, suddenly
an expert on everything and anything, Hauʻofa wrote *Our Crowded Islands*, an evangelical(!) tract on population control: "I assumed the role of social critic, a self-righteous prophet crying in
the wilderness, or more correctly a self-rightous public gadfly de-
tested or ignored by the powers that be. Up to that point, no well-
educated Tongan commoner had taken on the role of public critic
of the Establishment. I got away with it because I was protected
by the prestige of a Ph.D. degree and because I used for my arguments examples from the local culture and history as well as verses
from the Bible." Though Hauʻofa teases himself about this essay—
"capped with predictions of dire consequences should people dare
ignore what I said"—what abides is his deep affection for Tonga.

> Ours is a country of plenty: of yams, kava, sugarcane, pigs, tapa and
> mats. We derive joy from exchanging food with our neighbours on
> Sundays, calling passersby to share our family meals, drinking kava in
> an atmosphere of convivial fellowship with our friends, showering hos-
> pitality on visitors to our shores, caring for our elders and for those who
> have fallen on hard times, and offering first-fruits to our monarch and
> thanksgiving feasts to our God. Our songs are full of allusions to the
> beauty of nature. Our language is blessed with a great capacity for cap-

turing the most subtle shifts in mood and the most minute changes in the state of the sky, the wind, the sea and the trees. The bodies of our dancers are adorned with leaves and flowers and anointed with the perfumed oils of life.

Hauʻofa's *Kisses in the Nederends* has been called, not surprisingly, Rabelaisian. As Rod Edmond writes, "It is Hauʻofa's unique contribution to the Rabelaisian grotesque to have written a novel entirely about an anus." But, actually, the novel is about Oilei Bomboli, whose anus it is, and his heroic quest for cure, which perforce brings him in contact with the rest of the human circle in the Pacific. More, Hauʻofa's extraordinary eye for foible, and capacity to see it as human, evoke Chaucer as much as Rabelais. Finally, as in Hauʻofa's loving evocation of Tonga, one also hears a fear in the love, a terrible apprehension.

"I have lost my sense of humor," Hauʻofa said in an address he gave in Honolulu several years ago, speaking about Misima, the island where he grew up in Papua New Guinea. In the 1890s, Hauʻofa explained, Australian gold miners came, overwhelming the indigenous population. The local people appealed to their ancestors, but, Hauʻofa said, the ancestors did not help them. Later, with the approach of the Japanese in WWII, the Australians evacuated, though the Japanese never quite reached the island. Subsequently, when Australia reestablished its authority, there was a rebellion that ended in the public hanging of alleged ringleaders. In 1988, a new kind of mining began, with more powerful explosives and enormous trucks, devastating the land and fishing grounds. In ten years, Hauʻofa believes, mining will have leveled the island.

In his address, Hauʻofa followed this history with what he called an oral story he'd made up. (I'd heard Epeli tell this story several years earlier, I believe one of the first times he did so, in the midday heat in Suva over lunch at the Old Mill Cottage.) A kind of allegory, this oral story was also about an island, villagers, and mining. Here too the people prayed to their ancestors, nor were they afraid of death, because they had a heaven, down in a cave in the middle of a mountain, where they went as souls when they died. In the end, however, these villagers were destroyed by miners who, with their helicopters and explosions and digging, seemed to the people to be trying to blow their way to paradise. But these villagers were lucky, Hauʻofa said: moving into the cave, its mouth then sealed over by a blast, "they joined their ancestors."

Perhaps confronting the human has come close to overwhelming Hauʻofa's insistence on the absurdity of pretense and the consolations of laughter. Mark Twain, Jonathan Swift, Lenny Bruce—were they here, they might well recognize his problem. As noted, in Hauʻofa's recent essay, "A Sea of Islands," he's made one of his periodic efforts to be deadly serious, in this instance to discuss how Pacific Islanders should view their place in the world, how they can locate appropriately empowering metaphors. Given Hauʻofa's oeuvre, it seems he'll one day present a character who is a writer and works as a tenured professor. A fellow who cannot stop himself from wanting to save, if not the world, then the people of his region. Should this come to pass, one can only hope that the satirist will be gentle with his (only slightly more messianic) alter ego.

∼

On being a *fa fisi/palangi/haole/pakeha* reader of Pacific Island literature … In American law, "standing" refers to having a close enough interest to be permitted to enter into the legal process, having something at risk—past, present, future—that warrants participation. In appraisals of Pacific literature by outsiders, it may help to ask for the writer's sense of standing. *All literature is world literature? Books are written to be read?* Think of John Martin, who set down William Mariner's early-nineteenth-century account: by learning about Tonga, one is informed about the "infancy of human society" and "the incipient stages of the social compact." To lead the primitive into civilization, "from imperfection toward perfection," we must build "upon our acquaintance with [their] customs and modes of thinking …" (How hard to understand another culture: young Mariner was going hungry in Tonga, not realizing custom dictated that he was welcome at mealtime in any home.)

Today, when the bones of indigenous people are being taken out of museums and reinterred, this might be the moment to ask visitors to the Pacific who intend to commit art or criticism for a declaration of literary intent. Along with, perhaps, the agricultural declaration forms currently collected on flights arriving in Hawai'i. Not that anyone would be barred—no censorship, please! But, nonetheless, a brief statement of *cui bono*—to whom will accrue the putative benefit of this art or scholarship.

By way of example: in *Islands and Beaches,* a work of scholarship in which any vision of Marquesan reality is always tentative, Greg Dening says the book's bibliography "represents, in one sense, the extent of the dispossession of Enata [the Marqeusan people] … Whatever its limitations, it is a gift I give to the Land [of Enata]. I wish I had the wealth to bestow a copy of every item in it on the collective of Enata still alive. It would be some return for the pleasure that I have had in learning of their past."

Sensitive to prejudice/ridicule/hatred in both directions, Dening writes that there is "now no Native past without the Stranger, no Stranger without the Native." And, though "No one can hope to be mediator or interlocutor in that opposition of Native and Stranger, because no one is gazing at it untouched by the power that is in it," there is also no escape from this shared history:

> We have to write our history of the Pacific as the history of Native and Stranger Bound Together because we are bound together by that past reaching into the present. Who can change what was done? Who can return life or punish the dead? The only world we can change is that of the present of which we are a part. That world now has been encompassed by Native and Stranger alike. That world encompassed, the ways in which Native and Stranger possessed and possess one another is the object of our mutual and our separate histories.

⟋⟍

Outsider literature may be read as (if only inadvertently or occasionally) expressing not only imperialism or racism, but also aspects of the sometimes demonic power of storytelling. Currently, there's much discussion of the moral ambiguity of art, dating back to Joan Didion's famous remark, "Writers are alway selling somebody out" (which should perhaps have been more confessional), and, more recently, Janet Malcolm's reading of journalists as professional betrayers (again, perhaps insufficiently autobiographical).

What to make of these arguments? Hard to read Pi'ilani's memoir and concur. It's been noted that capitalism and the novel came of age together. Thus one might view fiction as an analogue of the corporation, a legal fiction freeing individuals from personal liability to facilitate entreprenurial—e.g., creative—behavior. Not that such freedom necessarily enhances the public good …

One *could* argue such concerns are only First-World decadence. But however we read, for example, *The Tempest* and its artist-king, the risks of literary magic are apt to persist even when Caliban holds the wand. Though Conrad is now deemed racist (by Nigerian Chinua Achebe), or at fault for not arguing imperialism had to end (by Palestinian-American Edward Said), what Conrad observed about the dangers of writing may still obtain: in the world of the book, "there are no policemen, no law, no pressure of circumstance or dread of opinion to keep [the author] within bounds. Who then is going to say Nay to his temptations if not his conscience."

Some years ago, Albert Wendt wrote, "I am not saying that ... the *papalangi* should not write about us, or vice versa. But the imagination must explore with love, honesty, wisdom, and compassion ... writers must [respect] the people they are writing about."

As a writer, I ponder this enjoinder. Possible? Desirable? One might settle for a literary map as complex as ... life. For some writers, this may entail remembering, as Hau'ofa writes, that when race is raised one must look to social class: "It is the poor who have to live out the traditional culture; the privileged can merely talk about it ..." *All* art has a politics. We also know, however, that those in the explicitly political arena—elected; self-anointed—despite their vision or virtue suffer the occupational hazard of oversimplification, withholding the also-true or the "personal," risk self-inflation, are task-oriented and so seldom find amenable the possibly mocking unruliness of art. May exclude the in-between, stressing the polarities Dening finds such a fraud. May be reluctant to concede that no one owns the whole truth, that they themselves are people of many parts. Further, are only *out*siders capable of cultural appropriation? *In Dreams Begin Responsibilities:* title of a book by Delmore Schwartz, a line as true for the indigenous, the autochthonous, or the aboriginal as for anyone else. It's hard, really, not to believe in *some* universals, despite so much insistence on *difference*.

If, as Wendt wrote, the Pacific Island writer's task is to present a map for his culture, that map might include the familiar: interracial marriages of the educated elite; that elite's success in the world as it is: no airbrushing, no bowdlerizing. *Complexity.* As Edward Said put it,

> No one today is purely *one* thing … Imperialism consolidated the mixture of cultures and identities on a global scale. But its worst and most paradoxical gift was to allow people to believe that they were only, mainly, exclusively, white, or Black, or Western, or Oriental … No one can deny the persisting continuities of long traditions, sustained habitations, national languages, and cultural geographies, but there seems no reason except fear and prejudice to keep insisting on their separation and distinctiveness … Survival in fact is about the connections between things … It is more rewarding—and more difficult—to think concretely and sympathetically, contrapuntally, about others than only about "us."

⌒

The Past and the Other are two of humanity's main preoccupations.
—Greg Dening

A recent conference on Pacific literature in Honolulu could evoke, for a *fa fisi* writer, Chaucer's *Canterbury Tales.* Coming from Auckland, Los Angeles, Apia, New York, the participants were on a kind of pilgrimage, and of course there were stories aplenty. And, inevitably, enough human foible to inspire fearlessly playful commentary—a fable by dead-serious clown Vilsoni Hereniko, perhaps, or the mordant verbal hula of "ono-ono girl" essayist Carolyn Lei-lanilau.

In its more formal aspect, the conference opened with a chant by Professor Lilikalā Kameʻeleihiwa, Hawaiian activist and determinedly revisionist historian, whose articulate bilingual presence immediately established one paradigm of current Pacific Island voices. Among the speakers were Marjorie Crocrombe and Albert Wendt, who'd both done so much to encourage and mentor Pacific Island writers, and the very number of Pacific Island participants created "critical mass," as panelists sought (sometimes new or indigenous) terms to appraise this literature. There was also this to note:

- In response to the plight of Hawaiians and Maoris, dismay on the part of Pacific Islanders whose nations are now again independent, or whose nations never lost independence (like Tonga).
- The obvious increasingly prominent role of Pacific Island women in academia and in activist politics, and the increasing sense of their own power.
- An air of hopeful expectation about the writing—the new maps—sure to come.
- A perhaps inevitable reluctance of some critics to grasp that any lens can distort or reduce as much as it magnifies, clarifies; or to understand that writers may subvert even a politically correct critic's imperialistic impulse. No one immune to, say, self-deception or hypocrisy, to use two hopelessly pre-postmodern words. Critics also sometimes in danger of understating the disparity in scale or risk between the artist's work and their own (all writing a text, no texts more equal than others).

As the conference proceeded, its setting in Honolulu seemed ever more central. The recent one hundredth anniversary of the overthrow of the Hawaiian kingdom (with the widespread if fac-

tionalized call for sovereignty). And the backdrop of contemporary internecine literary politics in Hawai'i, a multiethnic struggle
over who's really "local"—who's entitled to speak, it might be understood to mean. Exclusions and exemptions abound; competing Cinderellas, male and female, claiming the shoe fits.

The waning twentieth century, and Edward Said's insistence
on the contrapuntal—the combining of melodies. Fiji prime min-
ister Rambuka's "own story" of the 1987 coup, ghostwritten by
Fijian Stan Ritova and *palangi* Eddie Dean. A Rotuman educated
in Fiji and England teaching Pacific literature in Honolulu. Bare-
foot Fijian villagers with cane knives making copra; factory work-
ers in Suva earning twenty-five U.S. dollars a month. Anirudh
Singh's account of being tortured during the Fiji coup. A young
Samoan woman fluent in Samoan, English, and German just back
in Honolulu from several years in Europe, writing fiction in English to be published in Auckland and Hawai'i. A fourth-generation
palangi Fijian publishing a Micheneresque saga of his native land.
A part-Hawaiian ("Hawaiian," in contemporary parlance), having
lived on the "mainland" for years—New York, that is, seen from a
Pacific perspective—launching her neo-Micheneresque saga of
Hawai'i (with female protagonists and magical realism). These
multiple and simultaneous truths. With luck, some new Pi'ilani,
Dening, or Hau'ofa even now preparing to (re)tell the story.

Summer Swell

Waiting for waves. A collective despond, melancholy, dispiritedness permeating Honolulu, an interminable—two weeks of—lull. Not a hint of surf even over the July Fourth long weekend. "All dressed up and nowhere to go," as the song says.

"Any waves?" asks the Filipino workman, recent immigrant to Hawaiʻi. He's just being polite, seems almost determinedly oblivious to what's happening only a hundred feet away, at the beach beyond the intervening condos. No, not interested, though I've explained, loath to see him miss so proximate a miracle, that the waves vary from day to day, that the breaks are named, that we're waiting for a storm from the Antarctic, wind on water, to send swell thousands of miles to become rideable surf as it encounters the shoaling bottom and reefs of this south-facing shore.

"Waves?" I reply. "Nope; nothing." The workman smiles: something about being so compelled by the ocean strikes him as odd. Whatever: I tried.

Up before dawn each morning to paddle out, if need be just to sit and look. To get wet, as they say. Frigate bird soaring, then falling off down toward the mass of Diamond Head, forked tail open, each wing a lightning bolt. And, 'ewa, west, leg of a rainbow over here, the other leg toward downtown. Half a rainbow, more or less, with half a moon, more or less, up above.

Out to swim by the late afternoon, into the trance of breathing in, breathing out, slow, deep. One's consciousness itself rising and falling with the swell. Shoal of small sardines forming and reforming in the shallows at departure, return: a display of marine Aikido, so many ways to yield.

Day waning. Surfers have been sitting out in the lineup for hours, motionless except for an almost negligible lift and drop, lift and drop. Looking like pilings in the waning light, at long last approaching shore after sunset, shadows out of the blue/blue-black. Like cows coming home, moving very deliberately, or like birds giving one more turn around the banyan before settling in for the night, song suddenly stilled.

This continuum, concatenation, of sunrises and sunsets, Venus strong in the early night sky, Jupiter pulsing before daybreak. Solar days dazzling, overwhelming, dream state without beginning or end. Night: gibbous moon riding high, rivers, torrents of wind tattooing eddies and swirls on the skin of the ocean. Once, once I may have thought I controlled my water rhythms, my comings and goings to the *kai*, the *moana*. But it seems I was mistaken, was rather more like a cowrie or conch or even a bucket

of seawater: take me from (warm) ocean for too long, and I am …
lost. Getting back to water not so much option, desire, longing, or
hunger as absolute urgent need.

I return to the apartment to make notes, but my computer, so
functional a work tool, has begun to oppress. Truth be known,
there's no surfing the Internet: surfing is surfing; no aspect of a
network of computers is the ocean. It's a conceit, at best, a self-ag-
grandizing blurring of the essential, an assertion that does not …
hold water.

What is it about this warm ocean that can so obliterate trou-
bles, drain or absorb them, or itself be so absorbing that one's
drawn into its flow? "Easy," says the good doctor, grinning: "Today
the ocean's, say, seventy-five degrees; lowers your body's 98.6 for a
while, probably a good thing. Works to alter the hyperbaric pressure in your joints, too. Not to mention all the ozone." The doctor
laughs: a water lover, he has no wish, really, to try to explain what
he loves.

Henry David Thoreau, in *Walden*, wrote, "I left the woods for
as good a reason as I went there." A bit defensive, perhaps: a difficult point. Why not stay, having so baited the bourgeoisie for their
superfluities? And of course Thoreau's friends well knew how very
close to the comforts of home and friends he was at Walden Pond.
But possibly Thoreau was trying to explain the inexplicable. That
one can need or even love something and *still* find oneself giving it
up. More than once, heading from or to the Pacific or the mainland, I have shared Thoreau's feeling: "Perhaps it seemed to me I
had several more lives to live, and could not spare any more time
for that one."

For the moment, in any case, I'm here, where I should be. So many realities just *mauka* of the beach, in life on shore. Clinton v. Dole, the endless charade; new data on the (waning) ozone layer and global warming; the tale a man at the seawall is about to tell me about how he was hit by a shark in Micronesia. And, of course, about how he survived.

Out again to check the *moana*. Remembering a phenomenal swell a year ago, the endless circling wheel of incoming breaking waves, rising, driving, like the marvelous, incessant surge of a school of dolphins, still one more fin cutting the surface, over and over and over again. After several days in that swell, arms exhausted, daunted by so much inexorable power and my own inability not to go back out into it, there came a moment I knew I hoped their relentless assault would end. The swell itself at long last subsiding, as if it had had enough, for whatever reason. Leaving one to marvel at the incomprehensible distance between one thing and another. Between surf and no surf, or between sets and lulls.

A neighbor, an avid surfer, comes toward me. "See that," he asks, reading something in the barely breaking whitewater that I just cannot discern. "Swell's on its way."

"You sure?" I study the reefs.

"Absolutely. It'll be like first love."

I think it over. Not seeing even the hint of rideable waves, I'm inclined to disagree. "As I remember it, first love was ecstasy, despair, out of control."

"Right," my neighbor replies, grinning, as if resting his case. And then walks off, leaving me to ponder the comparison, and, willy-nilly, to appraise what if anything the whitewater portends.

Next morning, first light: still waiting. Pulse of yet another swell sure to begin again, as it has since not long after the start of time. But not yet. Just not quite yet.

Going to Samoa

Epigrams, Epigrams

Such are a few of the sights of the great south sea. But there is no telling all. The Pacific is populous as China.
—Herman Melville, *Mardi*

I was forty-nine—me, once always the youngest, now going on fifty?—and *On Water* was soon to be published. I'd been saved by writing about water, by spending so much time in and on it the previous ten years. Doing so, having to do so, despite the risk that too much might be washed away. But then, suddenly, I was obsessed with—incessantly reading, and eager to learn the craft of, the import of—epigrams, aphorisms, apothegms. Neitzsche, Leopardi, Joubert, Chamfort, La Rochefoucauld, Lichtenberg, Porchia, Kraus, Jabès, Connolly, Martial, Pascal, Wilde, Chazal, Valery, Cioran, Cunningham, Cannetti. It might have been a cleansing of the writer's palate, but if I'd once been drawn to prose out of an impulse for the comprehensive, for narrative, now I wanted my stories very short, if stories at all.

Of course writing is a form of argument, an attempt to convince the reader that one character or another deserves sympathy, that this is how the world works, is the language of understanding. But as I got into the epigrammatic, I was interested most in the argument's conclusion. The story a given, or excluded except as backdrop. The form's very brevity an argument: why labor the obvious? As for the sentiments expressed ... Well, my mood was wintry, an insistence on the human capacity for self-deception in the service of self-interest. And my language—oh, it was compressed, requiring attention, perhaps even a dictionary at hand.

But did I say argument? All this was peculiarly one-sided, left the reader little room for dialogue with the author, was almost pure assertion. Each short piece seemed to imply an unstated *quod erat disideratum*. Q.E.D.

Kronenberger, in his introduction to Merwin's translation of Chamfort, writes: "English is a natural language for [the aphorism]. Unlike French, English can dispense with both the definite and indefinite article, can let the genitive ride on the nominative's back, and prepositions dance at sentences' ends; and can thus be more pointed, more concise, more splendidly lapidary."

And it is true, for the writer as craftsman there is an enormous delight in working this form. But content and tone are something else. Martial, in the first century, and then La Rochefoucauld, in the seventeenth century, seem to have defined the form's air of disenchantment, the voice of fallen or banished aristocrat. The men's hut, male writers in middle age. As Joseph Epstein writes, "... the bone truth is that aphorisms, while they need not be bitter, are usually better for being so ..." And as La Bruyere argued, "no vice exists which does not pretend to be more or less like some virtue, and which does not take advantage of this assumed resemblance."

There was on the other hand the wistful Antonio Porchia, a real seeker: "Sometimes at night I light a lamp so as not to see." Of Porchia's epigrams, Merwin writes, "the distillate of suffering in some of the entries is pure and profound irony," but though I admired Porchia, he wasn't what I was after. Perhaps because, as Merwin observes, Porchia's was "an irony not of defense but of acceptance." No, I preferred, say, Lichtenberg, found overstatement well worth the risk: "A book's a mirror—when a monkey looks in, no apostle looks back out."

Martial and LaRochefoucauld. Playfully cruel. Acid. Scabrous: rough, harsh, indelicate. Passionate but detached, as if without illusions. Moralists moralizing. Punishing, implicating the reader with hard truths, forcing agreement. Self-absorbed, risking self-pity.

If the blues are an American idiom, in part because their formulaic laments are so confessional (Oprah Winfrey inevitably follows), epigrams are un-American. We believe in second chances, in mobility, insist we're a classless society. Our own most native epigrammatic impulse comes in the tag lines of country & western songs—"If the phone doesn't ring it's just me"; or, "She got the gold mine, I got the shaft." Amiable, and clever, but, as with the Porchia, not what I was after.

The darker aspect of words. As revenge, for example: Swiftian, the adjective. Which means? Well, Swift's Gulliver, back home from his travels, unable to abide the stench of humans. Avoiding wife and children by staying out in the stable with the horses, who remind him of Houyhnhnmland's four-legged creatures of true reason. Misanthropy: hatred, distrust, of the species. (The triumph of honesty over hope, some say.) In Swift's case, an equal opportunity–affirmative action misanthropy, misogyny included: "No wonder how I lost my wits; Oh! Celia, Celia, Celia shits." And, Swift wrote to Alexander Pope: "When you think of the world, give it one lash the more, at my request." On its "callous and insensible" posterior, of course.

Thackeray: "Ah, *Vanitas Vanitatum!* Which of us is happy in this world? Which of us has his desire? Or, having it, is satisfied?— Come, children, let us shut up the box and the puppets, for our play is played out." As I worked in and around this form, I'd phone friends to convey what I was up to. They'd laugh, ruefully, thought what they heard trenchant, tough. But later, several readers of the manuscript deemed my brevities, collectively, bleak, merciless, mean. Mean-spirited. Which left me disappointed, not in the news but in my friends. That is, I felt they were having trouble facing the truth. A bit late in the day, it seemed to me, for Pangloss, or to be getting squeamish. After all, it was Yeats who wrote, "Why should not old men be mad?" to think of "A girl that knew all Dante once/Live to bear children to a dunce." I wasn't old, yet, but I was having premonitions.

This, in any case, is what my friends were wishing somewhat more sanguine:

> *Not a complete cynic, he lies to others, but trusts them to believe him.*

> *There came a point when he realized traveling would not change him,*
> *but that coming home would.*

> *"You wasted your life," she says, flattering both herself and him.*

Another friend, a very good-hearted poet (more positive a soul than I, but also old enough to know that one has to work at being good-hearted), observed that epigrams could lead right into silence. "At the end of that road is silence," is how she put it. And this, I had to admit, had at least some merit. It wasn't simply that many of my compressions had to do with dying/death or foible/ folly, but that they were, finally—and despite all the play of words—a screed against language, against even bothering to continue the conversation. Which seemed to me at least one appropriate response to the world as I was experiencing it, like the behavior of the tribe that ceases to have children when its population falls below a certain level. Things were getting weird, without and within, no? When my sweet-souled poet friend, in any case, said that such epigrams could lead to silence, I responded, "There are worse things than silence."

If, however, I believed my epigrammatic writing had good cause, never did I not know that this was dabbling in a kind of black magic. (Not just the adolescent's bad behavior, or not even the coke freak's high, achieved with the understanding that the moment will be brief, the coming down rocky, the insights neon.) Perhaps all art's black magic—Prospero's wand. Often, cackling after hammering out yet another line, I'd think of the friend who became a compulsive writer of letters-to-the-editor. Long since, his brilliant calumnies have had little to do with changing minds.

About a year after I first noticed I'd become obsessed with the epigrammatic, I received a fellowship for a trip to Samoa: fallout from the water book. As I turned my attention to gathering materials for this return to the South Pacific, I noticed my addictive delight in the epigrammatic was beginning to moderate, though I did start culling what I'd come up with, preparing a short "final" manuscript. (A writer is someone who finishes things …) But the relentless hunger I'd had to write my compressions, as if they contained a mineral without which I could not survive, had abated. There is a tradition of eating dirt in both Africa and in the American South. Geophagy. Needing a certain taste or sustenance to the point of eating soil. ("The practice is found among peoples of low culture throughout the world," says the outdated *Webster's New International, Second Edition*, "and often develops an appetite or craving which favors idiocy ..." Or, according to a somewhat more recent definition, geophagy is either a psychotic symptom or a way of making up for lack of food, as in famine areas.) Not that I'd finished with the form—there was so much still to learn; I could spend years emulating Martial alone. Exposing myself to him, so to speak. Seeing what he brought out in me. But though I still wanted to pursue the craft of the epigrammatic, the sentiments the form seemed to induce in me no longer cried out to be expressed. And, or, I'd begun to tire of paradox, oxymoron, antithesis. Suddenly, inversions and apparent contradictions were too inevitable. Predictable, for all their surprises.

On my return from Samoa, when I once more made a decision to sit down at my desk, start *that* kind of travel—no passport needed—it was story, of all things, that was once again an imperative. Everything and anything, past and present, what I could remember or reconstruct, what I knew or could imagine of the lives of others, all of it suddenly seemed both accessible and vital to speak of. I began writing at a ferocious pace. And after a month of early winter rain, there came a time when, heading out for my double cappuccino at dawn one November morning, I looked toward the hills and saw a beautiful crescent cupping and illuminating the globe of the moon, fist of Jupiter pulsing just above. Saw, and wanted—oh, needed—to say so.

Honolulu International Airport

Sa moa of Samoa, as they used to sing.

Honolulu airport, waiting for the flight to Pago Pago (the *g* is "ng," as in *ping pong*). Many, many Samoans in the departure lounge, a surprising number of the visibly elderly, a dazzling number of children. More than a few of the teenagers with heads cropped and topknotted like Mongol horsemen, such theatrical fierceness undercut by the presence of so many infants and toddlers. Only one other *palangi*—Caucasian—in the lounge, a commercial fisherman returning to his job on the tuna boats.

In the airport bar, waiting for departure time. I am fifty, I am early as usual, and I am wondering if there is a mystery to my being in this place at this moment, an aspect or quality that should be obvious but that I do not see. Am I awake to my life, that is? The short, slight Filipino bartender, meanwhile, setting down my scotch, has asked where I'm going.

"Samoa?" the bartender replies thoughtfully. He seems to be pondering some larger issue. "Filipinos," he finally says, "Filipinos: little people, big islands."

I work on my drink, consider what he's said. Something essential may be emerging here. An evolutionary principle, a universal. But it's his play. I wait.

"Samoa," the bartender continues at last, smiling as if he's really on to something. "Samoa. Big people, little islands."

A Welcome Home

Richard calls again. He'd left a number of messages on my voice mail while I was gone, is enormously pleased I'm home even though he no longer lives in town. My being back in the country, however, the capacity to reach me, mean more than the words we exchange: everyone needs a baseline, and I'm Richard's. Which translates as that he trusts me to tell him when he's utterly out of control—as he often is. And/or to understand something of the world he came from—Boston, Irish lumpenproletariat. "Where'd you go?" Richard asks, a monologist's way of being polite. "Where the hell's Samoa?"

Just playing: Richard knows it's down there somewhere. But he called not to listen but to talk, to tell me how well his son's doing in first grade. Subtext? How worried Richard was that he'd messed up his son's life by not sending him to kindergarten or pre-school, despite all the computer games and toys. Or that simply by being himself he'd already consigned his son to a life more or less like his own.

Prototype for my character Mad Dog, about whose exploits I've written several times over the last fifteen years, Richard now lives in Reno. This after he left his rent-controlled apartment in Berkeley for a trailer on a hillside outside of Medford, Oregon, taking his then six-year-old and Rita, the wife he's never married, out of urban California to rural peace and quiet. Stocking up on guns, chainsaws, and a renovated '79 Ford pickup—purchased up there; Oregon has no sales tax—and running his credit card tabs to seventy thousand dollars, with little intention of paying them off.

Corporations sending unsolicited cards to an ex-convict on Social Security, to a self-diagnosed paranoid schizophrenic? What the cards purchased was quality stuff: a Ruger .357 Magnum stainless steel pistol with six-inch barrel; a five-shot mini-revolver using .22 Magnum slugs (something to put in your pocket and "carry around like small change," as Richard phrased it); and an AR15 semi-automatic rifle, civilian version of the M-16, with a 3 x 9 Bushnell adjustable scope.

Getting out of California had been occasioned by what Richard diagnosed, seriously, as male menopause—a biochemical imbalance, the symptoms of which were confusion, apprehensiveness, an inability to make decisions, and a ferociously inflated sex drive. His therapeutic regimen, self-prescribed, was crack cocaine, which non wife Rita got into smoking with him. "It numbs you," Richard said at the time, "which is good." Thousands of dollars up in smoke. Still, no addict, when he'd had enough Richard gathered the family and headed north. But Oregon didn't work out. Not only was there no waitress job for Rita—"no jobs, period," Richard explained—but then the police arrested Richard, twice, for shoplifting. In California, he was for years a Leonardo of filching, the Artful Dodger himself, supplementing SSI income with the occasional CD or filet mignon, just calmly walking out the door with whatever he wanted. But in rural Oregon? Perhaps businesses weren't doing well enough to write off inventory shrinkage. So there Richard was, forty-seven years old, 5'9", 240, no neck, wheezing heavily, making his appearance in court. His appearance. If you could get past his appearance. If he could.

Having been through the legal mill many times, Richard pled

guilty to a thirty-day suspended sentence. As he turned to leave the courtroom, however, the judge told him to take a lie-detector test. Richard had sworn shoplifting was out of character, but Oregon has a restitution program: the judge wanted proof he hadn't been shoplifting regularly.

A keen student of the Constitution, Richard knew this was doubly illegal. No one had informed him about the test before his guilty plea, and were he to flunk, it would constitute self-incrimination. Which left a firm believer in the Bill of Rights such as himself only one choice—to con the lie detector. Loading up on his prescription Xanax, a tranquilizer, "super for anti-anxiety," Richard's strategy was to "block a bunch of shit out. The stuff really works—you know without it I'm a nervous fuckin' wreck." Thus sedated, during the test he also made a point of not looking at the graph needle mapping his responses, and, recalling a brief course in Transcendental Meditation taken in prison in the late Sixties, visualized a black space to further calm himself. "I had no emotion in me, the Xanax cut it. And then I used my brain to bring down my heart rate, to make every question as literal as I could."

Though Richard beat the lie detector, clearly it was time to leave Oregon. Hence Reno. So many miles once again, but Richard continued to be plagued by his self-diagnosed male menopause. Which meant he was still in a period of heavy complaint, making him not entirely unlike many other American males. "My wife treats me like a turd," Richard said, again overlooking the fact that he and Rita had never married. "My son runs over me. The kid's a prick. I dread him gettin' up in the morning. He's got a fuckin' attitude. He don't go to sleep to damn near midnight, then he fakes sneezing or hiccups to piss me off. Takes him three hours to get to bed. I might go completely fuckin' nuts. I've never hit him, I don't let Rita touch him, nobody's going to do to him what happened to me, but he's spoiled rotten. Then he wakes me up in the morning. 'Get outta here, you little cocksucker,' I tell him. 'I don't like your little ass.' Tell you the truth, I don't know why I stopped beating people up, I really don't."

Richard said all this knowing I knew he'd been the primary parent raising their kid, that he still was, that he often had to protect their son from Rita's rages. "PMS," Richard said, matter-of-factly. "My mother had it bad too. But Rita? She's really herself only a couple of days a month." Recently, Rita struck their boy and left a welt on his face. Richard called the police, who warned her that the next time she'd go to jail. "I told her if she hit him again I'd turn her in for child abuse," Richard said. "She uses violence as if they're equals, rather than her being in a protective role. This is something she suffered as a child. That's just the way it is. That and the PMS."

Male menopause. As for the second-adolescence aspect of his malady, Richard wasn't impelled by a hunger for sex, but for contact. Back in California, before they headed north, one of their neighbors, herself on SSI and a crack freak, briefly seemed his true soulmate. "She was well read and intelligent," Richard said, "though it's a fact I sometimes mistake information for intelligence. Anyway, we really understood each other, even though she's nuts. She's the only woman I ever really listened to, but she's got an iron shield, she's been hurt real bad by people, she picks men who are easily disposed of. But for me it was all just fantasy. I mean, if she had ever said, 'Let's fuck,' I probably would have passed out. Really, push comes to shove I've always thought actual sex was dirty, rotten, ugly, a thing I'd rather dream about. I used to be pretty good looking, an interesting character, a literate ex-con; the ladies liked my act. You're aware of that. But I had a mother who knocked me around for fifteen years. I could've been a murderer, a Richard Speck. You know, Chicago, the dead nurses.

"Anyway, man, welcome home. Samoa? Fuckin' A. Glad you're back."

Stuck Inside of Mobile ...

After all, the only rule of travel is, Don't come back the way you went.
—Anne Carson

Oh Mama ... the ironies of travel. A standing apart from what has been. Perforce, a sense of multiple selves. Which can involve Flaubert's *"melancholies du voyage,"* whatever the erotics of departure. But in acting out Paul Fussell's "quasi-felonious" escape, what new self does one become? What tumult of selves? Especially when one sometimes wonders, "Am I going the wrong direction entirely, isn't it time to go east, east, back to the world of my childhood?"

American Samoa. In the South Pacific, halfway between Hawai'i and Australia, fifteen degrees south of the equator (at 170° W. longitude). Two-hundred-plus Samoans deplaning, greeted by many more hundreds of relatives, of Tutuila's population of thirty thousand. A community event, the plane's arrival.

In the cab to Pago Pago, the driver launches into a monologue about baptism. It takes a while to grasp, but we're talking the frisson of apostasy: he's repudiated the dominant Methodism—for more than a century at the heart of Samoan culture—for the Church of Christ out of Memphis, Tennessee. "LMS"—the London Missionary Society—was from a man, he argues, "but the Church of Christ is from Jesus." Making himself, to at least some of his family in a culture in which family is vital, pariah. A role he seems to savor, since it's occasioned by his possession of the true Word. As we reach the outskirts of Pago, he invites me to Sunday services.

Instant tropical depression. Pago brings one down. Stench from the tuna factories; the overcast, clouds cushioned by the

mountains; rain. The palpable air, in the oddly decrepit Rainmaker Hotel, of suspicion, menace. A staff person's response to in-
quiries an unspoken "Why me?" A phenomenally, almost humor-
ously, hostile look from one of the clerks. The intimation of a web
of intricate human connections. Intrigue, gossip, complexities of
status, face. Some Samoans know the Rainmaker can seem weird
to outsiders. A Samoan acquaintance from Honolulu phones to
see if I'm okay. "Many *palangi*s want to go home right away," she
tells me. Adding, abruptly, inexplicably, "Don't trust everyone."
Again, something almost comic in this unfathomable remark.
Quentin Tarrantino and David Lynch may enjoy a stay at the
Rainmaker, I tell myself, grinning.

Anomie also comes into my mind. *Anomie* used to be *the*
word in American social sciences. The kind of term Woody Allen
wanted to be able to throw around, that Susan Sontag could em-
ploy as effortlessly as teenagers mouthed "petting" or "making
out." *Anomie* having been bequeathed from Durkheim and Weber.
For them, when European society transformed from village to
urban, from *gemeinschaft* to *gesellschaft,* the individual became the
economic unit. Thus, the absence of shared social norms was an
essential aspect of industrial culture, anomie therefore at the heart
of what made America great, you might say, or what created so
many homeless. Choose one. Whatever American Samoa suffers
from, however, it seems unlikely that it is anomie.

Time, meanwhile, slows to a solid. Not just a time warp but a
time woof. Relativity disproved in the Rainmaker. One hour
equals several eons. Micro-events: a *fa'afafine*—markedly effemi-
nate male—waiter passes in the small coffee shop. *Fa'afafines:* for
writers from the outside, the beautiful Samoan woman *palangi*

men fall in love with turns out to be a transvestite, as in the stories of John Cranna and Graeme Lay.

For respite, happy hour at the yacht club in nearby Utulei. Happy year. A very tall and enormously overweight Robert Duvall, visiting Federal administrator from Washington, offers his saga. "Hey, I didn't want to carry an Uzi to work in the ghetto," inner city social programs having the only other available positions. Thus a stint in the American Pacific. Waiting for the freighter carrying his satellite dish and water bed, headboard with mirror. "You can tell I'm a bachelor," he says, grinning a Robert Duvall grin. Loading yet another cigarette into a plastic filter, making me wonder where he locates this prop in his vision of himself. (Homage to Hunter Thompson?) Saying that in Thailand during the Vietnam War he had a girl every night, "only had to pay for it five or six times." Planning on teaching in India, with four or five house girls. "I hear they have very good muscle control."

But what I'm experiencing isn't Samoa, is it? Only the odd no-man's-land that greets that misguided missile, the tourist. To break the Rainmaker's spell, I rent a car. An American solution, getting on the road, but the island of Tutuila is four by twenty miles. Still, I want to drive, as if going to the end of the line—all the way east to Tula—will imply a kind of possession. Miles "covered." Comes the question, how easily do we want a place, any place, to reveal itself? Isn't time spent the gift we give, the price we pay?

Meanwhile, before leaving for Tula I become obsessed with finding a map of Samoa, another kind of talisman. Another kind of fiction. Some way of giving (at least conceptual) shape to my experience. However: no maps at the Rainmaker. No maps at the Office of Tourism. No maps at the Wesley Bookshop. No maps on any floor of the vast government building, layers of offices and bu-reaucrats, monument to American Samoa's territorial status, nearly half the work force employed in "public service."

As if a map—or any such metaphor—could help anyway. "De-spair's a tree," my mother once wrote, trying out the notion that similitude can save. Hazarding the comparison, nonetheless, from bud to bloom, until in the poem's November she described "grief pipered from the bone, gold from the bough."

Maps, miles: later that day, no longer on the road, I'm visit-ing a young Samoan woman, friend of friends. A brave, funny, strong spirit, committed to archeology, Epi is determined to save Samoa's "material culture"—round stone hammers, adzes, fish-hooks—which the Samoan people seem to her not particularly in-terested in, this despite the importance of geneology and invoca-tion of *fa'a Samoa* (the traditional Samoan way). Epi's impulse to save what's gone is the stronger because she came back after col-lege in Hawai'i aware she'd changed, only to find that "Samoa had changed too." Trying to describe the discomfort of being between two cultures, Epi says, "I get lost in my heart." Unwilling to live with her family, as single women usually do, she has an apartment, her parents fearing she's become *palangi*fied, though they have a portable phone in their tin-roofed *fale*.

After lunch, in the heat, roosters crowing, acrid smell of garbage being burned, church bells ringing, choir next door re-hearsing the "Ode to Joy" from Beethoven's Ninth, Epi makes sure I understand I'm welcome to stay, then says she's going to nap. Sprawled on a mat on the floor, she closes her eyes. Intentionally leaving the TV on: after so many years in *fales* she likes the sound of other voices to sleep.

Myself ready to doze off, I see that the program happens to be from WGBH in Boston, on Nostradamus. Michel Nostradamus, sixteenth-century French physician, astrologer, famous for his hundreds of prophecies. Quatrains said to have predicted subsequent events, others, still being studied, their meanings obscure, thought to predict events yet to come. For example,

> *Mighty warriors spawned*
> *from lowly insects*
> *Fill the skies above the planet, third from the sun.*
> *Their goal is a home for brothers circling a dying star.*

This, some say, about space aliens …

Epi, sleeping. Missing her family. Reconstructing a lost Samoa. Her village now, at least for the moment, the global village.

Time Travel: Befoh's, Aftah's

... the already perilously thin line that separates memory from imagination ...

—Ofshe and Watters,
Making Monsters

Approaching Jack and Ann's, their house in Berkeley something out of Rip Van Winkle or *Sleeping Beauty,* front yard tumultuously overgrown, (perennial) morning glory rioting up the walls and onto the roof. Jacaranda, bamboo, alder, oleander, pitosporum, jasmine, myrtle, privet. Monterey pine, pear, dark-leaf plum; camphor trees out by the street. Not to mention several volunteer palms. Such deconstructing of an urban lot, this abetted reversion to Nature, surely violating several city codes. The apparent desuetude not only intended, however, but, as in a fairy tale, concealing treasures within—tendrils surging through the living room window, teeming bookcases, numerous canvases. Wit, music, the play of words. (The yard behind the house, with its birches, jays, squirrels, and rufus-sided tohee—"black hood, burnt sienna sides, white front, and black back striated with white," Ann says—being quite another domain.)

It's the Sabbath, observant Judaism chez Jack and Ann: we're about to have Scotch (with potato chips, raisins, pretzels, and grapes as chasers). No business on Shabes. Jack, in yarmulke and beard, chino pants and Oxford shirt, has set aside the *Chumash*— the first five books of the Torah.

"Tell us about Samoa," Ann says. She's more than entitled: the trip of an old friend entails the drama of departure and return. I've survived who knows what trials, have lived to tell the story, and of course as writer have spent my adult years persistently living to tell the story. But I duck Ann's request, ask after their marvelous grandson. Ann, you see, is a dedicated contrarian. Whatever I tell, her questions will inevitably—and rightly, I've had to concede—force me to acknowledge as also true something close to the opposite of what I recounted (and so argued). Among other things, Ann remembers that storytellers are often strongly drawn to what they most repudiate.

But even if Ann did not have an instinct for multifaceted truth and for the underdog and for the complexities of our attachment to the stories we tell ... And even if I sense that familiar, *un*writerly reluctance to reduce what I've experienced to story, lest in the telling I lose the original, words getting in the way ... (So much for writing being a process of finding out what one was thinking!) Despite all this, my evasiveness has another impulse. Back in California, despite a stay in Hawai'i en route home from Samoa, I've been sleeping eleven hours a night, napping frequently, struggling to get up in the morning. Reentry problems, I've told myself, a figure of speech that suggests I've been out in space. Spaced out ...

Leaving Jack and Ann's comes the question, Was it the trip or the returning that's done this? I take a quick look around. Could be the sheer density of lives in the San Francisco Bay Area: five million souls; nearly thirty million in California. (This must be what whale specialist Roger Payne terms "urbanicide.") The very numbers assaulting the environment, just the countless lights at night demanding correction. Which would take the form of ...?

All these humans in cars. As if our evolutionary function has been to pave the way, so to speak, for automobiles. Carrying the viral promise of them in our systems for millennia until they were ready. The car parasite impelling us to create more and more freeways, toward some ultimate moment when the last patch of open ground is graded and sealed, car horns all over the planet honking a four-wheel "Ode to Joy." En route to this alteration of Nature, the further cost of essential alteration of our own nature. Speed far exceeding our physical capacity, like the intricate impact of guns, or even clothing—i.e., no uniform, no dictators.

(Pig; shark; vulture; weasel; dog; worm; snake-in-the-grass. These creatures just doing their thing, actually. But that other epithet slithering back into our consciousness: human. Our technology—our own nature—the apparent enemy, so different from Boston's interminable slow Sundays in the early Fifties when I was a child, blimp eggbeating across the sky, the miracle of flight, yet the scale somehow still ... human. Even after two world wars, sixty-five million dead ...)

But *my* difficulties. I suppose they could stem from impending winter, days shorter here than down near the equator, early mornings before Daylight Savings pitch black when I head out for my morning double cappuccino. Light deprivation, now diagnosed as a health hazard, like so many things in our American twentieth-century lives. SAD, Seasonal Affective Disorder. But this too-dark darkness, the unsettling possibility of nature gone awry, the threat that winter will never end. No wonder God craved light to the point of creating it.

Or perhaps my mood's been caused by sight of "the homeless," so many visible poor in proximity to such wealth and frenetic consumption. All in a land of vigorous selfishness and sense of injury—voters bitter about taxes, illegal immigrants, "second-hand" cigarette smoke. Millions of citizens on prescription drugs for "depression." (Pharmaceutical companies, backed by the government, having won the War on Drugs.) White males, that endangered species, pro-handgun and pro-deportation, voting Republican in the midterm election. Terminally conservatized by such phrases as "safe sex" or "Year of the Woman." (Less than 39 percent of the electorate vote: Congressperson Gingrich's mandate against the "counterculture"—that is, nearly everyone not himself—speaking for something like 20 percent of eligible voters.)

How overlook John Wayne Bobbitt's penis? Or ads in the sports page of the *San Francisco Chronicle* for surgical "penile enlargement, penile lengthening"—oh Penile Nation! Dr. Rothenstein promises, in a pitch for "Men Only," that "Most Patients appear as if they have doubled in size …" Not that he intends to solicit homunculi … Penises in America: AIDS, something like half the gay or bisexual males in San Francisco are HIV-positive. Rape, date rape, molestation: the penis as evil, as death. Penile, penal: one million citizens in prisons and jails. (A subsequent *Chronicle* article reports that operations to enlarge the penis are "unnecessary in all but a tiny number of men …" (Male fans of Italy's World Cup soccer team, beaten in the finals, apparently suffered a decrease of testosterone by game's end.)

San Francisco: long the home of postmodern body "modification"—tattooing, piercing (nose rings, eyebrow safety pins, lip studs, labia rings), now into branding, the kiss of fire. Everyone getting ready for Halloween. Forget the O.J. and Nicole masks. Small beer, Halloween being *the* annual holiday here, fueled by years of gay liberation, a polysexual camp sensibility, and psychedelics. As actor Brian Freeman is quoted in the morning paper, "One always wants to do drag for Halloween, but how much pain is one willing to tolerate …" (Think of the thousands of Brian Freemans, the last few centuries, all the incarnations of those four syllables, iterated infancy through senescence, BrianFreemanBrianfreemanBrianFreeman, not to mention the homonyms, *Bryan*

Freemans abounding, until you achieve "One always wants to do drag for Halloween ...")

"Pull yourself together," people used to say, perhaps responding to what seemed self-pity. Not an enjoinder one hears these days: changing cosmologies. Pulling myself together, in any case, I do think my problem could be memory. But not, I hasten to add, "recovered memory," the term now used for injuries belatedly remembered in therapy by former children throughout this great land. Most of the memories consisting of alleged sexual abuse by the patient's parents. My own memories, for better or for worse, being no more than the data of some fifty years on the planet, so many specifics rushing back into consciousness after the odd obliterations of travel.

Memory. Traveling, I'd forgotten too much, more than I should have risked forgetting. I'd forgotten winter: soaking rains, gutters overflowing, leaks in the garage, wet running shoes drying by the heater, windshield wipers slapping, how much I could appreciate being warm, the attrition of exposure to cold. Suddenly memory seemed fragile, puny, hopelessly inadequate: nothing would stop the passage of time, the loss of what had happened. What would even a pyramid evoke, really?

The obliterations of travel. Part of the thrill, no? Presuming a confidence we'll make it back to tell the story. Or travel as a rehearsal for death, good-byes all around, trial run for the Ultimate Voyage. A striptease: How much can you shed? The erotics of pseudo-death: think of S&M asphyxiation freaks, consenting adults with hands round each other's necks, *squeezing*, while struggling to say, to hear the Other say, "Fuck me (almost) to death. Please."

Or, it could all be stress, a word that, like *impotence,* has magical qualities: to say it is to risk it. Talk about "better left unsaid" … Stress as a way of life: our era of "stress management." The danger: that we are incessantly mobilized for fight or flight. Worry in the form of "what ifs" can cause what Dr. Robert Eliot terms "chronic vigilence," which by increasing levels of the chemical cortisol raises blood pressure, "slows metabolism, increases fat and cholesterol," and "diverts energy from the immune system."

To counteract this pernicious syndrome? A detailed "master plan": "Know what you want, how you plan to attain it, how long it will take you, and when you will work on it," argues Tim O'-Brien. "Uncertainty is the cause of much of the anxiety we experience." It's also important to identify sources of worry and resolve them, with "outside help," if necessary, as well as to be positive. (Question: Odysseus's master plan?)

On my return from Samoa, I talk to a man who's been sick for a month. Exhausted, unable to stay awake for more than several hours at a time. Joints aching. None of this visible, of course, and he has the misfortune of being married to a strong, attractive, successful, loving career woman who believes, more or less, that character is health. Meanwhile, seeing numerous doctors, he hears of "chronic fatigue syndrome"—the invisible-but-diagnosable-incurable, fears the shoe fits. Fears also that in stopping smoking as he approached fifty he's undermined the precarious balance of his immune system. His not an entirely unusual contemporary American medical moment. At last, however, he gets what he hoped for: a clear diagnosis. The bad news being that he has brain cancer.

Which reminds me. Years ago, I stopped smoking on the premise that the damage I'd caused myself was reversible. This was medical propaganda at the time: *back to normal*. Now, however, they have something called "pack-years." Tell my physician how many cigarettes for how long, and he'll calibrate just how much permanent damage I did myself.

Winter. Stress/SAD/illness. I have a friend who says her father was in a rage the last few years of his life.

"The last few years?"

"Yes."

"What was he so angry about?"

"That he was going to die."

Mikey, meanwhile, just turned eleven, runs on the beach for hours, bounds like a gazelle, canters with an awareness of his own cantering, this secondary sweet savoring of his own being-in-the-world. Narcissism, I suppose, or a kind of informed cluelessness. *No Fear*, says the Nike ad. Mikey throws the ball back to me hard, fast, far. *His* knees and back will not ache in the morning.

Mikey. He likes chess, plays with nonstop chatter, bouncing, humming, tapping, whistling, not all of this conscious, but not all of it inadvertent, either. Some of it from what TV argues kids his age are like, the loveable airhead; some of it from TV's apotheosis of trailer trash and ghetto dissing. Some from the hormones, surging. In chess, he savors watching me put my queen at risk, savors even more taking my queen, having worked on the cool way one simultaneously picks up the opponent's piece and sets down one's own in its place. Deft, expressionless. Then getting up to do the football player's slow-mo end zone moonwalk, fist and forearm pumping one, two, three times.

Eleven in America. And here comes … an insolent facial expression. A smirk, a sneer, a snotty radiating knowledge that adults don't know as much as they claim they do. That adults know very little, actually. Mikey and I look up a word in the dictionary: *condescend.*

Mikey: how tell an eleven-year-old, suddenly aware of cost as status, that money really doesn't matter. Or, that it does, but doesn't. Or, the eleven-year-old at breakfast, reading the sports page, making fartlike sounds, cheeks puffed out, while he studies the box scores. That is, he's happy. Or, when he asks about phases of the moon, I think of the model of the solar system I had as a child, adjustable metal arms leading to each celestial body. I remember too living in the Cyclades half a lifetime ago, stars throbbing, reading Robert Graves's Greek myths. Mechanics or miracles, then: which to convey to a boy who's already using the word *bored* with a vengeance, but who's nonetheless himself still a kind of miracle, a truth obscured by the mechanics of helping to raise him.

I remember … I remember that in 1972, nearly twenty-five years ago, my brother came out to visit, and each afternoon we threw a football. I would have been in my late twenties, was running five miles a day, had in an essential way at last become myself, physically, whatever metabolic apogee the genes had in mind. It was one of those extraordinary northern California summers, high and clear and blue and temperate, fog sitting off the Gate across the bay, even more beautiful to a native of Boston, given the absence of high humidity, the absence of any threat of rain. An extraordinarily benign environment, it seemed, this long before all the more recent fires/floods/earthquakes/overcrowding/Death of the Defense Industry—before this round of California as dystopia. Oh, I knew about the Donner party, had read Nathaniel West, seen *Citizen Kane,* had been part of the Sixties nova, crash and burn.

And yet, still California had a freedom, bounty, and mobility that to immigrants from the eastern seaboard was miraculous.

California, in 1972, to me was not-death, though as it turned out there is plenty of death in California. I would never have said it then, or even thought about it in such terms, but I not assumed but felt either that I'd live forever or that times like this could go on and on. *Felt:* to articulate such an idea would already have been to undercut it … And though my brother would never have agreed, had it been stated, this was a time and place that would have made him want to believe. Which may explain why he never moved out here, despite so many visits over the years, despite his love of the climate and terrain and their contrast to the eastern seaboard, perhaps preferring not to be in the position of having a dream tested, denied. That day, in any case, our passes were strong and accurate, right on the money, as they say.

The past. The future. From an Associated Press story, "nearly six in ten … [Americans] believe the world will come to an end or be destroyed and a third of those think it will happen within a few years or decades … 44 percent believe there will be a final battle of Armageddon, with true believers … called into Heaven." This article provokes me to ask myself what I think. Clearing my throat, I respond: "I believe the world will end some day, though in a future too distant for me to comprehend. Recorded human history is very brief in the grand scheme of things. And of course for many peoples their world ended—they died: that some other part of the planet continued on probably did not console. But in the short run, for the entire Earth? My guess is something on the order of the kind of inversion we saw in *Planet of the Apes.* Nuclear war or overpopulation, then some 'corrections.' A rogue virus. As for

Heaven and Hell, before arriving after death at a long line of rotis-series—how can there not be a Hell if so many people have imagined and feared it?—I want to add this ... My real fear is that Hell is what I and a number of others made of the here and now. Thank you for asking."

Fate of the species aside, how to view this, that my sometimes interminable moment here on earth is moving, *poof!*, toward conclusion? That the I-who-I-am won't be here forever. That this fellow who pumped iron yesterday (those biceps, those sit-ups, those abs!) and who made love yesterday (that erection!) will utterly cease to exist. Some years ago, writing about my mother's dying, I came across a passage in Freud that would have made me howl with derision when I was young. Now, despite all its flaws, the passage stays with me, stays with me:

> The attributes of life were at some time evoked in inanimate matter ...
> In this way the first instinct came into being: the instinct to return to the
> inanimate state. It was still an easy matter at that time for a living sub-
> stance to die ... till decisive external influences altered in such a way as
> to oblige the still surviving substance to diverge ever more widely from
> its original course of life ... before reaching its aim of death. Seen in this
> light ... the theoretical importance of the instincts of self-preservation,
> of self-assertion, and of mastery greatly diminishes ... What we are left
> with is the fact that the organism wishes to die only in its own fashion ...

～

"Billy Pilgrim has come unstuck in time," writes Kurt Vonnegut in *Slaughterhouse Five,* his masterpiece about the incineration of Dresden. Past/present/future bombilating in on Billy Pilgrim without regard to the conventions of "realistic" Forties war fiction à la Norman Mailer or James Jones.

Unstuck in time: I've never been much interested when people

speak of previous lives—in the Egypt of the pyramids, ancient
Greece, that kind of thing. Perhaps because for my people much of
the past was spent wandering the desert or in bondage; and then
too I'm into water. Though, of course, it would have been something to have been there when Moses parted the Red Sea. (I also
want to go on record as saying I have "nuthin' 'gainst no Pharaoh,"
if I may paraphrase Muhammed Ali on the Viet Cong.) So, speaking as a private person: no particular interest in past lives. I like my
miracles more down to earth: this flower, that butterfly.

On the other hand, however: you could also say I *currently*
have a number of lives, not past, but present. Time traveling. I am
this kind of a tourist, this is my baggage. You can't go home again?
Oh, but you can, and I'm afraid to. To go home is not simply to re-
visit a place one once lived, to view with different, older eyes what
was, but to risk reentering the life one could have lived, that never
stopped: watch that kept ticking whether or not one looked at it,
garden that grew with or without witness, radio station one dialed
away from, broadcast of course still continuing. To go home is to
take on what one repudiated or declined, whatever the price, so
one could be … something that, it seems, had no final form short
of death. To that point, always the chance for retelling. For deathbed conversion. For reading the voyage differently, from the point
of view of—what else?—destination. The curse of story, if you
think about it: the possibility, probability, of revision. Of
infidelity. (Though I do love Grace Paley's brilliant "Conversation
with My Father," the narrator's insistence—arguing with her dying
father—that story will and must keep changing … as long as
there's life.)

Perhaps I'm tired because since leaving Boston thirty years
ago I've been living two lives simultaneously, like the man with

two families, two wives, two homes, two sets of kids. Newspaper accounts always focus on the web of lies, the treachery. Deplorable, of course. But think also of the remarkable strength of the perpetrator.

The paths not taken. Consider the Sixties, which briefly offered—required—an entirely different perspective of government/authority/war/drugs/money/status. Millions of people for a long moment lived that life. Where then did it all go? Those people that they were? How integrate that into the present, what new story do they learn to tell?

Traveling. Staying. The writer in his study, at the ergonomic desk made by a friend. Bookcases of different shapes and sizes cheek by jowl, most of them inherited from local bookstores as they renovated. The books—accumulation, filing, and (even) reading of them—part of a writer's life. One case of the unread, the to-be-read. A mixed fiction and nonfiction alphabet. A separate section on biographies of writers and books about language or writing. A section on water—with a subsection on surfing. A section on sex, lying, death.

That sweet gum tree—called liquid amber—out my study window, rust-red leaves against cloudless blue sky. My neighbor's backyard, his house an endless renovation. His wife, who years ago died, young, of cancer. The clan of feral cats near his decrepit garage. The book *The Plenitude We Cry For* by Sarah Appleton, published in 1972, a "record of one season's growth of a horse chestnut tree in 1964 in Northampton, Massachusetts … The form is a series of notes imitating the stages of the tree's growth: reflective, concentrated and elliptical, exploding, enumerative, suspending, dispersing, in summer spare and mechanical."

Traveling, staying … Part of the reason I became a writer was to say, "This is what happened, this is what otherwise would be missed, unmentioned." Only slowly naming what was right in front of my eyes. Writing is in some ways like travel—both are transformations of the self, functions of a hunger to be different than one is. As Peter Conrad argues,

> Discontent and restlessness dictate our language. There is no poetry without metaphor, and metaphor transforms things into that which they are not … It grants the wish of every noun to be an object other than the one it names, it speeds every verb on its way out of sight; it is imagination's excuse to go walkabout … it caters to our secret need to shed encumbrances and pass on.… To have more than one life is the craft of the actor, and the dexterity of the traveller. It is also the desire and rage of the artist, who no matter what identity he inherits will long to be different, and no matter what portion of the earth is home to him will want to be elsewhere.

Nonetheless, how many chances to do we get to do something with full commitment? To travel is, perhaps intentionally, to dissipate, stray, wander. So much of my life, my job has been close attention to the here and now.

My copy of *The Plentitude We Cry For* belonged to my mother. Her sustained commitment to poetry and accumulation of books from which she could learn are part of her legacy. So, once again, I pick up this book, for it has much to impart, and, reading, move to this writer's mind, to a tree three thousand miles and twenty years away and ago. As my mother wrote,

> *Why should I travel, where should I be,*
> *Dream is my distance, and it comes to me.*

Portents

All roads seem to be leading to Samoa. This one leads to a beautiful house in the country so near to the city that only rock stars, upper professionals, and entrepreneurs can afford it. This woman, a computer magnate, met her Samoan husband in college in the late Fifties. Suffered wife beating, left him, raised their son alone. Went through the Sixties as a hippie, got into computers early, made it very big.

Her grown son, in the hot tub under the redwoods. Took a recent short trip to American Samoa to see his father, was very glad to return after two weeks. "They're like overgrown children there," he says, looking up from the tub, "like *Lord of the Flies*. I don't tell any of my cousins my address; they'd all come over to live. One cousin was beaten to death there. They're very violent people, horrible to children and dogs. It's a total nightmare."

A week later, I meet a professor of medicine from Stanford Medical School. A French citizen of Vietnamese-German descent, a brilliant surgeon who lived in Western Samoa for ten years, he received both a *matai* (chiefly) title and the Legion D'Honneur for his commitment to the Samoan people. Patients from other countries in the South Pacific flew into Apia—not otherwise their destination of choice—to have him perform surgery. And how had this talented citizen of the world liked his ten years in so remote a place? "Oh," the doctor told me, "I love Samoa."

Biology in Samoa

Q: *So you now have your parents' furnishings?*
A: *No, I sold them off again. I am not attached to things like that. In any case, I need this room for meetings, so it is better that it is bare. My father is dead. My mother is dead. Why should I cling to their furniture?*

> —Burmese dissident and Nobel
> Peace Prize winner Daw Aung
> San Suu Kyi, *New York Times*
> *Magazine,* 1996

In the late nineteenth century, Britain, Germany, and the United States were vying for power in Samoa (a struggle that led to the present American control of the eastern islands of the archipelago). Germany annexed Western Samoa in 1900, only to lose it in World War I. Hence the many German names in Samoa, the ongoing interest of Germans in Polynesia. Thus it was no surprise that in Honolulu I met a German biologist whose area of study is the South Pacific. She was in town to deliver an academic paper, and we were both invited to a small dinner gathering in a dorm at the East-West Center. The biologist, on crutches, was accompanied by a younger man—assistant, protege?—who deferred to her, almost in reverence, it seemed.

At table we surely might have claimed to be reflecting the East-West Center's ideal: our Fijian host, a Samoan graduate student, the two Germans, a visiting American writer. The biologist had spent time in Samoa, it turned out, but had little good to say about either the country or her host family, dogmatically playing the expert before going on tell a story about how she was given the only

Western bed in a *fale,* which her drunken host one night, forgetting she was there, tried to climb into. Somehow, the story conveyed that the biologist saw no anomaly in her being in the *fale's* one bed, honored guest in a family home, instead of in a hotel. That is, she had every right to be in Samoa, to its hospitality, every right to say what she felt. Was, if pressed, to be congratulated for saying it, speaking as she was as a German who'd made a point of expressing her shame of fascism. All this with and despite her manifest disability. Her companion, meanwhile, with attentive silence, gave full support.

Predictably, the evening ended badly: the Samoan graduate student left in outrage, after several years in Hawai'i already long since fatigued and/or dismayed by outsider versions of Samoa; and the Fijian host was in tears to see such rancor at his table.

That night, leaving the campus and back in my apartment near the ocean, I marveled at the idea of travel, of goals—the comparative study of language, for instance—that could set, say, a disabled German academic in motion. I had no answers, but resolved to examine my premises if I continued to wander the Pacific: what I thought I was up to; what I imagined had carried me so far from home; what kind of stories I'd return to tell.

Restless that night, I again picked up William Weaver's translation of Italo Calvino's dazzling *Invisible Cities,* in which the young Marco Polo tells the aging Kublai Kahn tales of places he (says he) has seen in the kahn's vast empire. One city Polo describes is the essence of a young man's dreams, at which the fellow arrives, however, in old age. Another city, Polo says, knows departures, not returns.

Initially, Polo could use only pantomime to communicate

with the khan. Still, when, over time, Polo's "words began to re-
place objects and gestures ... first exclamations, isolated nouns,
dry verbs, then phrases, ramified and leafy discourse, metaphors
and tropes ...," then "communication between them was less
happy than in the past ..."

At one point in their ongoing dialogue,

> Marco Polo imagined answering ... that the more one was lost in unfa-
> miliar quarters of distant cities, the more one understood the other
> cities he had crossed to arrive there; and he retraced the stages of his
> journeys, and he came to know the port from which he had set sail, and
> the familiar places of his youth, and the surroundings of home, and a
> little square of Venice where he gamboled as a child ... that what he
> sought was always something lying ahead, and even if it was a matter of
> the past it was a past that changed gradually as he advanced on his jour-
> ney, because the traveler's past changes according to the route he has
> followed ... the foreignness of what you no longer are or no longer pos-
> sess lies in wait for you in foreign, unpossessed places.

Finally, when the khan points out that Polo has never spoken
about his home, Venice, Polo responds that all his descriptions
have been in some way about it. "'You should then begin each tale
of your travels from the departure, describing Venice as it is, all of
it, not omitting anything you remember of it,'" the khan says. But
Polo demurs: "'Memory's images, once they are fixed in words, are
erased ... Perhaps I am afraid of losing Venice all at once, if I speak
of it. Or perhaps, speaking of other cities, I have already lost it, little by little.'"

Medea in Samoa

I was in my late forties, walking down an unpaved sand-covered road in Rotuma, a very small, quite remote South Pacific island below the equator, population several thousand, the morning already sweltering and incredibly humid, lots of flies and mosquitoes in the profuse vegetation and fallen fruit. There seemed to be no one around, and as I walked on in the heat, expecting no vehicle to pass and hearing none, there being only a handful of motor vehicles on the island, a song came into my head, a song I learned as a child, perhaps because I was on my way to speak to the students at the island's high school. Or perhaps because I walked to school when I was a child (often in snow and sleet, wearing galoshes, gloves, cap with earmuffs, and overcoat, but also sweating it out in Boston's inexorable presummer or postsummer heat and humidity), and there I was, once again walking to school. Whatever the reason, I was headed down that road in Rotuma, singing,

Oh Madele, oh Madele, pray tell me where's your home?
"My home it is in Switzerland, it's made of wood and stone
My home it is in Switzerland, it's made of wood and stone."

Very Tyrolean, the chorus: "Yo-Ho-Ho, tra-la-la-la ..." Get out your dirndl, your lederhosen.

Two years later, I was again in the South Pacific, this time in Pago Pago, sitting out by the pool at the Rainmaker Hotel, dark clouds approaching, rain not surprisingly just about to be made. A visiting Australian professor, speaking of a sometimes contentious academic, said, "She's the Medea of the Pacific." The professor's bitter hyperbole startled—Medea, of course, murdered her own children. Further, given the setting, one was awakened for a moment to the distance in space and time between us and the fourth-century Greece of Euripedes. (There is, nonetheless, Futa Helu's Atenisi [Athens] University, very present in contemporary Tonga, built on a curriculum of the classics. And, as Marshall Sahlins has pointed out, ancient Greece was already a fault-filled reconstruction by the Renaissance that so invoked it.)

In any case, as the professor and I sat, now silent, watching the approach of and waiting for the rain, the whole moment, oddly, put me in mind of Rotuma two years before. Of walking in the heat and singing a song from a childhood then nearly half a century and a third of a planet away.

Glabrous (A)

A. *Glabrous*: smooth; having a surface devoid of hair. Years ago, when I first thought of shaving my head, I was in New York visiting my married friends Chris and Bess. This would have been in late '71. They were early gentrifiers in SoHo, loved being down near Canal Street among the painters and filmmakers, the all-night bakeries, the factories—just a few blocks from Little Italy. Chris was already collecting art, his friend Lewis's tiny, postage stamp–like canvases being his favorites. To Chris, Lewis had the added allure of being artistlike: Lewis just could not hold a regular job, for years depended on friends to help him out when no one was buying his paintings. Could have sold some paintings, but died a thousand deaths every time he confronted having to actually part with one. Would be depressed, silent for days. Really, though he never quite said so, he wanted only famous collectors and museums to buy his work. And/or, he simply wanted to keep it all in his studio. Chris, who'd invented himself out of a family from the lower depths, who'd become physician, lover of fine things, black belt in Kung Fu ... despite these truly heroic acts of self-creation, Chris thought artists to be not at all like himself. Loved Lewis for both his tiny paintings and for his apparent inability to function in the "real" world.

Lewis had other qualities. He "inherited" a small monkey from one of the junkies and winos who crowded the stoop at the foot of the stairs to his loft. At first the monkey was company, a kind of friend, good for long days alone, but then Lewis began to get interested in monkeys in general, entered both the Manhattan subculture of people into monkeys and the vast literature on monkeys, moving then to obsessive reading about evolution—arguments about the degree to which we're like or unlike various simians— finally arriving at the issue of primates and lab research. Haunted by nightmares of the cruelties inflicted by humans on monkeys, Lewis became an antivivisectionist activist and stopped painting. ("Far out," as people then said.)

Bess was a film editor, loved fashion, rock and roll, marijuana, sex. Indicated some interest in an affair, but I was then observing the Boy Scout code: I'd have had to be "in love" to bird-dog my friend's old lady. Not that it was easy to overlook her: she was a kind of Wyf of Bath—lusty, and she also liked to talk about sex. She also showed me that affection some women reserve for men they'd like to sleep with but may never get around to. Always a twinkle in her eyes when we spoke. Thus, so many years ago, when I mentioned I was thinking of shaving my head, her response was pure Bess.

"You better remember what a shaved head looks like." She produced one of her high-gummed double-entendre grins. Mock lascivious but lascivious. "Need I labor the point?"

I just listened.

"So," she continued, "with that kind of look, you'll always have to be 'on.'"

Even allowing for Bess's sexual gusto, a shaved pate does make a strong statement, which must be, so to speak, supported. Nonetheless, years later, tired of feeling deciduous (and well before black players in the NBA made it a commonplace and white America, trotting close behind, made it a fashion), I took on the various stock evocations of the time: Yul Brynner, Telly Savalas, (Marvelous) Marvin Hagler, Zen priests, prisoners of war, professional wrestlers, patients in chemotherapy, skinheads, the strong-man in the circus. The convict Magwitch in the Forties film version of *Great Expectations.* G. Gordon Liddy. Not surprisingly, people came up with still more reference points: "You look like Gurdgieff with a surfboard," said an old college friend, speaking of the Russian guru in Paris in the Forties. I myself often remembered a counselor at camp when I was ten, a man of perhaps fifty, which then seemed unspeakably old. Wally Dow. He was in superb shape but had not a hair on his body. Or, none we campers ever saw.

Tonsure: noun and verb, the ritual shaving of an acolyte's head as preparation for entering a religious group or order, the correlative of promised spiritual change. Possessed of a shaved head, an order of one, I became something of a walking Rorschach test, or, a heightened version of the Rorschach test we always are to others, received various strong responses, certain of which came to be predictable.

An elderly Japanese-American woman in her tiny barbershop on Wailae Avenue in Kaimukī, on Oʻahu, shaved my head. "You're lucky," she told me, hand trembling as it held the straight razor. "Your skull. Very beautiful."

"Thank you," I responded. "But may I ask a question? What makes it beautiful to you?"

She paused, thoughtfully, as I looked at her in the mirror. "No dents," she replied.

A woman I'd gone out with years before bumped into me, said, "Oh Jesus, what happened to your head?" She was some thirty pounds heavier than when we'd shared a night or two, had yielded to gravity perhaps more than she was able to acknowledge. I bit my tongue.

Bess was right. You had to be "on." A male friend wanted to tease me, but I tired of the joke. "God gave me a choice," I said. "Shaving my head, or being you."

People also seemed obsessed by the mechanics of personal hygiene, felt free to ask. At Waikīkī, once, when I came in from surfing at dawn, a potbellied tourist in porkpie hat, Bermuda shorts, *aloha* shirt, white socks, and loafers—surely a look of intentional self-parody, perhaps what tourism is really about—stood watching me shower off.

"Can I ask you a question?" he finally began. I stared, water dripping. "How often do you need to shave it?"

I thought it over. "Tell me something about yourself," I responded, which made him turn and walk away, though I suppose it could have led to stories I was unprepared to hear.

"Are you with the tattoo group?" a concierge in a hotel lobby once asked, some kind of convention in town, apparently. A peculiarly appropriate question, actually, since I'd begun to identify with Melville's Queequeg (Ishmael's Marquesan soulmate in *Moby Dick*) and his tattooed pate.

Two final categories of response come to mind. Some women were impelled to lay hands on my head, making the visual tactile. A bit intrusive, but not all bad. And, within my own range of perception, in high winds I occasionally experienced the sensation of having very long hair, a kind of postamputation ghost limb phenomenon. I also had to watch out for heat loss and sunburn, which led me further into hats than I'd thought of going, but that's another story. Suffice to say I was sure this new fellow was me, just as I'd known it when I first grew a mustache more than twenty years earlier. Whatever the feedback, I'd have mustache and shaved head for the duration.

In time, I grew used to seeing my shaved head both in the mirror and in the mirror of others' responses, learned to handle such constant overexposure. Doing this, I was accomodating to a visual inevitable that could also be a virtue, as had, say, Dolly Parton. Appearance equals destiny, something like that.

In this period, I made a three-month stay in Fiji. By then there were videos in Fiji, but not yet TV. (Thus, little familiarity with Michael Jordan's recently shaved head.) My first week in Suva, it seemed everyone was staring at my forehead and above. I learned, however, that if I raised my eyebrows several times—causing me also to wiggle my ears—the result was a warm smile from both children and adults. (I later understood I'd stumbled on a standard Pacific gesture of affirmation.) Given that there were some seventy thousand people in Suva, not to mention villagers in on the smoking buses for the day, I nearly herniated my eyebrows that first week.

Many of the kids also said to me as they stared, "American Shaolin, American Shaolin?" Timing is all: a martial arts movie with that title was playing in town; the protagonist shaved his head to begin his apprenticeship in China. I made no verbal response to this question, simply smiled and raised my weary eyebrows yet another time.

One night in a small restaurant across from the Morris Hedstrom store by Nukubulau Stream—The Wedge, it's called—I was waiting for my dinner, rereading Hau'ofa's *Kisses In the Nederends,* laughing out loud at his absurdist Pacific. I'd have fit right in to Hau'ofa's crazy saga. Was fitting right in. As I read, the waitress came by with a second Scotch: a large Fijian fellow at the bar had sent over a drink. I saluted him, reciprocated by asking the waitress to give him another Fiji Bitter. It occurred to me the Scotch was an expensive gesture, given the Fijian economy. Inevitably, the man approached my table.

"American Shaolin?" he asked, looming above me.

I'd had enough. My eyebrows ached. "That's correct," I said.

Smiling, he offered his right hand, which was enormous, and connected to an enormous forearm. I offered mine, and we started to shake. I should have guessed—within a millisecond he was applying pressure, not in itself painful, but frightening in conveying what might follow.

Truly, necessity is the mother of invention. I looked up at the Fijian. "Please," I said as sincerely as I could. "I don't want to have to hurt you." I'm alive to report that he dropped my hand, smiled, went back to the bar. There is a God.

There was also, in Suva, the suggestion that someone who "looked like" me was in town. The first time I heard this it was from an expatriate professor at the University of the South Pacific,during a cocktail party. His remark interested me only a moment before something else took hold. If I thought about it at all, I filed it under *C* for crudeness of perception: all shaved heads look alike, etc. Another time, however, down on Victoria Parade by Lucky Eddie's and neighboring drinking spots, a *palangi* I'd never met walked up and spoke as if continuing a conversation we'd been having earlier. When I began to demur, then to insist we'd never met, the *palangi* was clearly sure I was teasing him. A double in Suva? What the Germans call a doppleganger? It seemed improbable, and there was already much in Fiji that to me was stranger than it appeared, some essential foreignness only masked by the overlay of Western toys. Heading on to Tonga and then Rotuma, I thought no more about it.

Two years later, during a stay in Apia, capital of Western Samoa, I was not particularly surprised when children called out *"ulupo'o, ulupo'o"* as they saw me pass. No hair. There were perhaps one hundred thousand people on the island. In a week or two, if I wandered around as usual, and if I spent some time at the public market and in the bars, most everyone would have seen me; I'd become unremarkable. Or so I reasoned.

But the kids were also calling out something else besides *ulupo'o*. Not "Brew-know, brew-know," as I first heard it, but, I began to gather, "Bruno, Bruno." I asked around. Bruno? *Tupa'i* Bruno, it turned out, to grant the man his *matai* (chiefly) title, an American who brought a circus to the South Pacific each year, a (very) tattooed man who tamed lions, sawed women in half, performed magic. Who, like me, had a shaved head and a mustache. Small world. As I made my way around the island of Upolu, I felt like MacArthur returning to Corregidor, waved to the laughing, cheering children I passed, smiled benignly in a way that for me evoked the kind of pose the Pope might strike in his travels. Not merely tolerated, but began to enjoy the attention.

Several days before leaving Apia, on my way to start a pub crawl at The Love Boat with Samoan novelist Sano Malifa (who once traveled around the United States by Greyhound, inspired by Jack Kerouac), I passed two young boys. They stared at me—the usual—but then one said to the other, *"He's not Bruno."*

How cruelly flat the tone of his voice. Not Bruno? No magic—

no feats of courage? No lions to tame? No applause—no chiefly title? No full Samoan tattoo, hip to thigh? In and of myself, truth be told, I was little more than a stranger in a—to me—strange-land, a place that could hardly be expected to take the measure of my life as writer/friend/teacher/son/sibling/lover. In Samoa I was, above all, an outsider far from home. So now, though I'd been liberated from the burden of a stranger's identity, "Not Bruno" felt like a kind of loss.

Subsequently, back in California, I had reentry problems. There but not there, out of synch: not quite myself. This despite abundant evidence of the life I'd led for so many years—cottage, bookcases teeming, silver '78 Camaro, people I knew, cared for, loved. Who knew, cared for, loved me. All that defines who one's been, who one will be in the morning.

Still, disoriented as I was, this question emerged: If "not quite myself," who might I be? A question that, thanks to my time in Samoa, I could begin to answer, if only by elimination. That is to say, I'd learned I was not Bruno.

Holding Elections

Q: What do you call a Samoan wearing six-guns in Texas?
A: A Western Samoan.

The contemporary Pacific. A bar in Apia, Western Samoa. John the Rotuman telling me another joke. More time warp: off-color jokes, drinking, everyone smoking like chimneys, all of it as unimpeded as it was in the United States twenty years ago. John's an architect, speaks Rotuman, Fijian, Hindi, English, Samoan. Refused to cut his hair and beard for eight years as an ongoing pledge against his grandmother dying. John and other patrons in the bar gazing into middle distance as they lip-synch the words of Patsy Cline's "Crazy."

In Apia, I also meet Tasi Malifa, an attorney of perhaps forty, educated in New Zealand and later at Harvard Law School—the first Samoan there?—where he studied constitutional law with Alan Dershowitz. Tasi, in this island nation with a population only a fraction of Boston's, happens to know my Cambridge, the particulars of my late adolescent map. Harvard Square. Mass Ave. Sleet. Mount Auburn Cemetery. Slush. The T. It pleases me, elicits a smile, the thought of Tasi in Boston.

Apia. I'm oddly ready for it: just prior to departing Hawai'i for Samoa, at the urging of Epeli Hau'ofa, who's visiting at the East-West Center, I come to his rooms to hear twenty-five-year-old Samoan Sia Figiel read stories from a work in progress. A large and determinedly theatrical woman of enormous force, just back from living in Europe for several years, Sia performs—chants, in a mix of Samoan cadences and MTV—a lover's vision of Apia as a kind of Pacific Penny Lane. Her great affection for Apia's foibles blends with the irony of one who has already traveled very far. Clock tower, market, cab drivers, schoolgirls—landmarks and dreamers of Apia—I see them the first time unwilling to clear my head of the tone of Sia Figiel's vision. Remembering Epeli beaming after Sia finished, clearly hoping that this young woman would realize her talent, become part of a new generation of Pacific Island writers. (Sia's parents, I later learn, live outside Apia, her mother Samoan, her father Polish from Baltimore, a career Navy man, and among other things the first American sumo wrestler.)

Meanwhile, at Le Godinet's Beachfront Hotel—Derek, the proprietor, tells me he once performed as a singer with Harry James—I'm rereading Albert Wendt's powerful novel *Pouliuli*. Being in Samoa is changing the book for me. To begin with, I now realize that in Samoa Wendt is *afakase,* half-caste, no matter how Samoan he is in or to the outside world. Distinctions within distinctions, not surprisingly. Also, I now have some sense of the scale of the universe Wendt was describing, the island of Upolu's one hundred thousand people, its fifteen by fifty miles.

Pouliuli is the story of a Samoan village chief, "the seventy-six-year-old titled head" of his extended family, who wakes up one day with a feeling of revulsion for all he has been—husband, father, lay preacher, successful farmer. "Even the familiar smell of his *fale* and relatives now repelled him." His determination to reveal his clan's hypocrisy to itself is the engine of the story, and leads, inexorably, to tragedy for him and others.

Pouliuli, published in 1980, makes it clear Wendt had read his *King Lear,* Sartre, Camus. This cross-pollination of writers and readers, their ongoing (often silent) conversation. Which makes it, perhaps, not so surprising that early one morning in Apia, between the intermittent thunder storms with their heavy rain, as I walk down Mulinu'u Road toward the bustling public market, the idea for a novel comes to me. I have to pause to let the idea in, stand staring out past the Japanese-financed breakwater. It's late 1994, elections approaching back home.

The idea? President Clinton goes on TV to deliver a speech written without the knowledge of his advisors or spouse. "My fellow Americans," he begins, pausing for effect, "I did inhale." He goes on to say he's slept with a number of women while married, really cared for some of his lovers, and that he nonetheless loved—and loves—his wife: "One can love a spouse and still be unfaithful," he says, "and many of you know this kind of thing to be possible, or to speak to some similar complexity in your own lives." He makes this confession, President Clinton explains, because he's sick of hypocrisy, of all the lies he's told. The young man he once was—and has resolved again to measure up to—is that Sixties dope-smoker who imagined he'd be a mole in government, a semisecret agent who'd betray the rich and powerful to be true to himself and "the people."

I envision my story as a fable, the narrative voice incantatory: "Once upon a time, a time of computers, of Prozac, of Safe Sex and many dildos, of huge flying ships and an alienation from nature, a time of the death of nature ... once upon a time there was a president of the United States ..."

What will become of my president, I wonder, as I walk into town. Will he step down, lead a crusade, a march across country? How can it not end badly? Is that an imperative of the story, America's karma—*Easy Rider* redux—or a result of Albert Wendt's brooding influence?

In any case, this is what writers love, something to chew on.

Perhaps to really try to tell. An epiphany in Apia, occasioned by Albert Wendt's powerful book and my own cargo of memory. And, perhaps, by another of John-the-Rotuman's jokes, President Clinton calling the president of North Korea to ask, "Hey, when are you going to finally hold your election …"

As for my own cargo of memory, it's not quite that I want to be free of it. If enlightenment for mortals comes from escaping memory, as in Buddhism (the gods, of course, remember everything), I've condemned myself to a writer's life. That is, to a transformation of memory in words even as I'm left with a keen sense of the artifice of the process. As Stephen Owen argues, memory involves the writer in a "secret compulsion to repetition … Something is not content simply to be and to have been, but must try to be again and again, and never successfully and finally."

Nonetheless, I've been up to something of this sort for considerably more than half my life. And believe in the pleasures of working the medium more than Owen (says he) does. I can even remember, I think, the actual moment of choice, confronting yet one more extraordinary Dionysian force in the Sixties, opting to describe rather than yield to it. I'd met the neo- or pseudo-Gurdgieffian Alex Horn, felt I was confronting the dilemma of either joining his group or recounting what I'd seen there. Which at the time seemed the far more conservative decision, if all I was capable of.

Of course it's late in the day for me to arrive in Samoa carrying so much psychic luggage. Could it have been a bit like this for Robert Louis Stevenson, already world-famous in 1890 but trying to outrun tuberculosis when he settled in Western Samoa at age forty? Stevenson extended his life some four years by coming to and remaining in the tropics, but surely, as he laboriously built his estate in the highlands above Apia, surely he must have had the sense that he'd already moved into a kind of recapitulation.

Stevenson, his name and presence, like Margaret Mead's, still reverberating, oscillating, in Apia. His face on postcards. Some Mormons, they say, are developing his estate as a more extensive tourist destination: just the kind of time travel Kurt Vonnegut would savor.

I visit neither Stevenson's grave nor his home. But I do know the requiem Stevenson composed for himself, learned it as a schoolchild in Boston, some forty years and eight thousand miles before Apia:

> *Under the wide and starry sky,*
> *Dig the grave and let me lie.*
> *Glad did I live and gladly die,*
> *And I lay me down with a will.*
>
> *This be the verse you grave for me*
> *Here he lies where he longed to be*
> *Home is the hunter home from the hill*
> *And the sailor home from the sea.*

Anthro

A joke from my childhood. One native says to another, "Quick, take off your blouse, here comes the *National Geographic.*"

Having read if not the *National Geographic* then his Margaret Mead, British philosopher and radical (and later Lord) Bertrand Russell wrote, in *Marriage and Morals:* "We are told [that Samoans] when they have to go upon a journey, fully expect their wives to console themselves for their absence." Bernard DeVoto, who also read Margaret Mead, had this thought: "The more anthropologists write about the United States, the less we believe what they say about Samoa."

Saved

Deploring the passing of traditional cultures, searching for a vanished reality, anthropologist Claude Levi-Strauss wrote of Brazil in the Forties, "What travel has now to show us is the filth, *our* filth, that we have thrown in the face of humanity." Ah, born too late: "What I see is an affliction to me; and what I do not see, a reproach." And so Levi-Strauss travels, "groaning among the shadows ..." A clever man, however, he also knows that in earlier eras he himself would have had different eyes, would have seen ... less, perhaps.

Levi-Strauss also knew there were other hazards of travel, had read his Chateaubriand: "'Every man carries within himself a world made up of all that he has seen and loved; and it is to this world that he returns incessantly, though he may pass through, and seem to inhabit, a world quite foreign to it.'" As Levi-Strauss asked himself, "Was that what travel meant? An exploration of the deserts of memory, rather than of those around me?"

Collecting treasure as I wander in Samoa, I notice I'm holding on to the six-page flyer given to me by the proselytizing cab driver when I first arrive in Pago. At odd moments, sifting through my acquisitions, putting packets together to mail home, I take yet another look at this flyer, wonder what I imagine it has to teach me. A church out of Memphis, Tennessee. A city evoking the ancient capital of Egypt, in a state that took its name from the conquered Cherokee. All of which evokes in my secular, rock-saturated mind Paul Simon's extraordinary song "Graceland," in which he and his son are heading through the Mississippi delta toward Elvis's home.

This activist church, its flyer "Truth for the World" and radio broadcasts in Africa, the Caribbean, and the South Pacific. "The Devil is real and his evil influence is powerful." Since no mention is made in the New Testament about instrumental music, "it would be sinful to ADD it to the singing …" Obedience to the Gospel. Being lost. Salvation. Righteousness. Faith. Repent. Satan. The Holy Spirit.

"Dear Reader," Louis Rushmore asks in the flyer, "Are you saved?" Something to ponder, I conclude more than once as I come across the flyer in my pack in Samoa, when I find it among my things on my return home. *Saved.* The washing away of sins by baptism.

Powerful, this language, this appeal, but ultimately wasted on me: long since, I've had enough conversions for a lifetime. Perforce, I'll go with the commitments I've made, honor them as best I can. As the Hebrew God said, more or less, I am that I am. It's me that's him. Small *h* in *him,* for yours truly.

Glabrous (B)

No man has of himself the notion that other people have of him, espe=
cially those who know him little.
            —James Boswell

While in Fiji that first trip, I met Australian land-developer David
Charles Miller, his wife, Else, and their daughter Sachan. David
spotted me in Suva one day, immediately referred to me as his
cousin-brother. David was in his early forties, had lost quite a bit of
hair, had a thick moustache, and outweighed me by perhaps seventy-five pounds. But still, one *could* see the family resemblance,
and in Fiji everyone has many uncles, aunts, cousin-brothers.

Blessed with Australian bonhomie and directness (intermittent only because he also had incredible wit and a quite canny aspect—missing no nuance, even when knocking back yet another
Fiji Bitter), David was prospering in Suva. Unlike so many expa-
triates, he could successfully work with the mandatory Fijian partner in each of his enterprises. David also knew quite a few *ratus*, the
chiefs, hosted parties for them, seemed to have a gift for being
around them. I asked his wife how he did it. "I expect it's because
he knows his place," Else replied, laughing. A cosmically Zen laugh,
I might add: David had spent years promoting a religious group
(devoted, he explained, to "giving of energy to purify spirit").
Though no longer with the group, David seemed to understand
people very well, or perhaps it was simply himself he understood
very well. Whichever, he had a gift.

Once, at his office on Amy Street in Suva, I met an American who with his wife had built a small resort in a remote spot with some beautiful cottages on the beach, a *ratu* of the local village their obligatory partner. One day, apparently, the chief's son said he had to use the dive boat to transport a sick villager around the island to the medical station, quite a long way. The American protested: there were hotel guests to take out diving. A fistfight ensued—was it the American's wife the *ratu*'s son hit?—effectively terminating the partnership. In the middle of nowhere, *ratus* were the law, were in many ways above it. When David bought the American's share of the resort at a fire-sale price, I asked how he planned to handle things better. "Oh," David said, as if it were obvious. "The *ratu*'s son *had* to use the boat. That's the Fijian way. I expect the best thing is have two boats ..."

My cousin-brother, his wife and daughter. They showed me great hospitality in Suva, and David was brilliant, though some of his projects made me uneasy: he was opening up beautifully isolated places. Still, he was no worse than the face of the wave of the future; it all was going to happen sooner rather than later, with or without him.

Several years later, I had the pleasure of seeing David and his family in California as they passed through on vacation. In the course of their visit, I told them about my trip to Samoa, and about my doppelgänger. I should have guessed: David, Else, and Sachan know Bruno. Bruno Loyale, that is. American citizen, seventh-generation circus, mother and father in Barnum and Bailey's, speaks six languages, a dancer, magician, lives in Matautu, in Western Samoa, stayed with David, Else, and Sachan for weeks and weeks when his circus came to Fiji. David, at the urging of a friend in

Samoa, was Bruno's impresario in Fiji, brought the circus over. Had Bruno's lion, babboons, miniature horses, and several Samoan animal keepers out in the backyard during Bruno's stay. Later, Else and a friend traveled with the circus aboard ship to the remote islands of Wallis and Futuna.

And yes, Bruno has a shaved head and mustache. "But no, Tom," my Australian cousin-brother David explained, Else nodding in agreement, "Bruno really doesn't look a bit like you."

So Was It True?

Still, one kind of wants it answered, once the question has been framed: were the Samoans Mead studied into free love and adolescent sex, or was this notion, as they say in Hawai'i, *shibai*—phoney, bullshit.

Desultorily drifting toward the heart of the matter, I stumble on a clue. It's Sunday morning in Apia, after a long Saturday night's pub crawl. A woman from the last bar—she lives near the hotel, seemed to have been trying to make some kind of connection when we spoke the night before—now approaches, walking down the street as I stand looking out to sea.

We chat, watch yet another pickup truck go past, cargo of women and girls dressed in white heading for church.

She laughs. "Angels on Sunday," she says, smiling, significantly silent about their behavior those six days of the week it took the Good Lord to flesh out His creation.

I have that smile and those words then, as clues. And this, from Sia Figiel's *Where We Once Belonged:*

> "Go back to where you came from, you fucking ghosts! Gauguin is dead! There is no paradise!" …
>
> Palangis were confused when they heard such words—most of them were shocked, shocked that someone recognized them doing what they usually did: Peeping-Tomming for a past, an illusion long dead, long buried in museums of their own making. They were ashamed and looked down, buying ulapule or coconut earrings from an old woman out of guilt.

Souvenirs

The souvenir may be seen as emblematic of the nostalgia that all nar-
rative reveals—the longing for its place of origin. Particularly im-
portant here are the functions of the narrative of the self: that story's
lost point of identity with the mother and its perpetual desire for re-
union and incorporation, for the repetition that is not a repetition.
The souvenir seeks distance ... in order to transform and collapse dis-
tance into proximity to, or approximation with, the self. The sou-
venir therefore contracts the world in order to expand the personal.
                                        —Susan Stewart, *On Longing*

En route to Honolulu from San Francisco, three hours into the
flight. My game plan was to stop in Hawai'i for a few weeks, get in
some surfing and spend some time at a conference on Pacific literature, then head down to Samoa. On the plane, several hours still
to go, restless as usual, a self-diagnosed aristo liking not very much
the cheek-by-jowl democracy of mass transit (and lacking the Frequent Flyer Miles to upgrade), I extricated myself from my seat.
Not surprisingly, I found other loose marbles at the rear of the air-
craft. (Hawai'i, in one of its aspects as an American conquest, is a
kind of Vegas; all sorts of mainland human flotsam wash up on its
shores. New lives for old, distance and rebirth.)

Standing near the toilets and galley, a man in his early thirties
quickly rendered a version of himself as New Yorker in California,
young James Caan with a touch of DeNiro. He began by saying
how tired he was. Why? Because he'd been running back and forth
between two girlfriends, one of whom was a whore, a prostitute,
that is, but who loved him, the other a virgin—except for being

with him, presumably. Needless to say, she also loved him. The whore bought him gifts—car, clothes, vacations—while he used her money to buy things for the virgin. Through this narrative, he kept grinning a Caan/DeNiro I-know-I'm-a-heel-but-I'm-loveable grin. This grin, however, statistically works best cross-sexually and/ or with someone you've only recently begun sleeping with. (For writers, there's that initial moment when your lover thinks everything you've written is a masterpiece. This before she begins to look for the autobiographical truth—i.e.: betrayal of her, before you met her—in your fiction, prose now scrutinized through the lens of direct self-interest …)

Perhaps ten minutes went by with this fellow's sexual saga. When he seemed on the verge of winding down, still eager to kill time, I asked what kind of work he did. "Narcotics agent," he responded, grinning sheepishly—winningly, he intended—and then launched into a story in which some guy at the Presidio, a Marine, not knowing he was a narcotics agent, "disrespected" him, which led him to set the man up on a drug bust, etc.

"That's horrible. You ought to be arrested," I interjected.

"You don't believe me?" he asked—a remarkable nonsequitur— and pulled out a billfold, flashed a badge. "Look real?"

Maybe, but he was already on to a riff about how in New York his father and brothers were "connected. In the business. Organized crime." Everyone but him in the family being in the Family. His father not wanting him, the youngest son, to be a criminal. Of course not: in *The Godfather* does Marlon Brando want Al Pacino to be a criminal?

"That's how it is; I'm a cop. Even so, I do anything my father asks, anytime. He tells me to get down on my knees, suck his dick, I get down on my knees, suck his dick."

"Come on, your father never told you that."

"Yeah, right, but I mean, I would if he did. Understand?" No *d* in *understand*. And then, abruptly changing the subject, making me wonder what substance he was abusing, he said, as if reading my mind, "What's your favorite drug?"

"Are you crazy? I'm going to tell a nark, or someone who says he's a nark, my drug preferences?"

"Oh, I'm not shitting you, I'm a nark, but you and I are just talking. I'm sincerely interested." More young James Caan.

"Fortunately," I say in a loud voice, looking around for cameras, "I can say for the record that it's been years since I took drugs. I trust this moment of our conversation is also being taped."

"Don't be paranoid. I believe you. But, on the other hand, when you did use drugs, which ones?" Here he seemed more into Harvey Keitel.

The theatre of American storytellers. Garrulous strangers. Instant (apparent) friendship. Shitkickers, bullshitters, salesmen selling themselves, getting sold. Motor mouths. Whatever fills the void. Once, on a flight from San Francisco to Hawai'i, I sat next to a man who radiated a desire not to talk, as did I, both of us determinedly absorbed in our magazines, books, drinks, food. Loud silence between us. At hour three, however—clearly the near edge of eternity, a trip that might never end—both of us broke down. Which took the form of exchanging an initial few words about destination in Hawai'i, and then two hours of nonstop conversation—political prisoners with amobarbital injected into the carotid artery have said less than we did—which lasted until the beginning of the long final descent to Oʻahu. In all that talk, that apparent exchange, neither of us ventured his name: it was understood the words were to get us from here to there. No more, if no less.

As for this flight, the nark and his presentation of self? Fuck it, I thought: deal me in. ("Travel and travellers are two things I loathe"—wrote Levi-Strauss in *Triste Tropiques*—"and yet here I am, all set to tell the story of my expeditions." Four hundred pages' worth, actually.)

"Dexedrine was the rage when I started college in the early Sixties," I began. My roommates and I started with grass, for possession of which you could have been "expunged" from college at that time. Later, I tried LSD, opium, and DMT, as did nearly everyone else I knew. In the Seventies, self-interest with glitz: I was into coke, but only when it was free. I loved burning someone else's money, loved the hard clarity, hated the coming down. In any case, coke only when free—that was where I drew the Just-Say-No white line."

He laughed. "Very funny. I'm going to use that one."

"Thank you. But I want to add something serious. I stopped using the coke, free as it was, because one day a friend shared some just as I was on my way out the door to shoot hoops. Of course, at the court my heart was racing. I couldn't play. That really pissed me off. That was the end of coke for me."

"Just like that?" the nark asked.

"Yup. Just like that. I loved basketball, wasn't about to give it up. But there was something else going on. The marijuana and the psychedelics, as opposed to the coke, really did offer a vision of an entirely different set of priorities. I stopped using them not to 'clean up' my life but because of a kind of failure—I couldn't handle the distance between the drug and nondrug worlds. Those Sixties drugs took me to a set of values too benign or true or insightful for a person like me to live by; they insistently suggested changes I was unprepared to make. Should have made, I suppose. Coke was different—simply more of the 'real,' heightened, hardened."

"Heavy, man, that's really heavy," he said, with apparent sincerity.

"Whatever. Enough of the past. For the record, I want to state that now and long since it's single malt whiskey, and only when I remember to make myself drink it. For medicinal reasons. I have a doctor who prescribes it."

"You're trying to tell me no current drug use?"

"You don't want to hear about my doctor who prescribes single malt whiskey?"

"Hey, my thing is drugs. You absolutely sure you don't use them at the present time?"

I felt I was letting him down. "Now that you mention it, I had some dental surgery a few weeks ago. The Percodan was wonderful. Phenomenal. Not worth the surgery, but almost. Now I understand why friends of mine used to rave about it."

He grinned. "Think you'd like some?" he asked.

"Some what?"

"Percodan. Percocet, actually."

"Great. You're a narcotics agent and you're offering me drugs?"

"Percocet. I got lots of it, suitcases. Vicodin too. I'll get some for you, soon as we get into Honolulu. Tell me where you're staying."

Just as he said this, there was a jolt of turbulence, and the captain's voice on the intercom told passengers to take their seats, stewardess forcefully shooing us away from the galley. And that was the end of it: I didn't see the agent—or nonagent, whichever—the remainder of the flight or as we deplaned (he'd said something about FAA regulations, having to check in and retrieve his pistol before boarding and after landing). He was gone, the American way of intimacy. White noise.

When the turbulence during the flight began, I went back to my row as ordered, wedged myself in, accidentally-on-purpose whacking the seat of the traveler in front of me, who'd reclined as far as he could. But nothing doing: he didn't budge.

Rustling around in my bag, I pulled out some Herman Melville, that extraordinary singer of prose songs about the Pacific (and, as young author, in *Typee*, playing The Man Who Lived With Cannibals, an appropriator of secondary sources and teller of tall tales, still only genius-to-be). One of Melville's books I'd brought with me to reread was not about the Pacific, though it too is set on water, on a steamboat on the Mississippi. *The Confidence-Man*, coming near the end of Melville's great decade-long torrent of writing before his long literary silence. As Michael Rogin writes, it "was the last piece of Melville's prose to appear in print while he lived, for thirty-five more years." An April Fool's saga about appearances and deception—impostors, swindlers, hypocrites, frauds, and dupes on the pilgrimage of American life—*The Confidence-Man* is obsessed with trust, or its impossibility. Melville, as Rogin argues, coming to terms with both his father and his nation.

I was lugging books with me to Samoa because I needed to be sure I had them available—for pleasure, or against possibly hostile environments. As for *The Confidence-Man*, I brought it both because of Melville's writing about the Pacific and because his career can be read as a cautionary tale—arguably the greatest American writer both losing his audience and at risk of losing his mind. Finally, I brought *The Confidence-Man* with me because my mother, in her midsixties, a few years before her death, had published a collection of poems that took yet another wry look at the implacable universe, leavening hard truths with detail of nature closely observed, with fidelity to the memory of her husband, and with a love of the music of language. *Something Further …* this volume was called. The title coming from and an homage to the last line of Melville's *The Confidence-Man:* "Something further may follow of this Masquerade."

My mother inscribed the copy she gave me: "For Tom—this Masquerade."

Water and Writing (cont.)

Edmond Jabès, an Egyptian Jew who lived in France for many years (he died in 1991), in relentlessly innovative prose questioned the essential nature of text, form, the divine. It was typical of Jabès to argue that the notion of freeing oneself through writing is absurd: every syllable "unveils" another bond.

Water, it happens, is also one of Jabès's obsessions. For instance,

Driven mad, the sea, unable to die in a single wave.

What is sung by the sea
men in turn sing
to the sea.

With nothing left to invent God drowned in Himself.

Pondering the mystery of language, Jabès suggested that a writer at work is like an angler. Pen as rod, fishing the empty page for language.

In from surfing one day, as usual making notes after a shower, I see the process somewhat differently: the writer as alchemist, yet again transmuting water into words.

Kona

Urged

The water sounds like jets—
   like maybe a hundred jets
      taking off or taxiing around.

And the rumble is distant,
unseen
staring back
from the black
haze.

The waves are big
that's known.
But how big?

One doesn't know
on a moonlit night
with only the
creep of the cool,
deep blue,
breeze
sliding over
sinking in.

It's deep,
    and rumbles,
as deep as
the horizon is sharp,
        deeper than I know
how to feel.

Oblivious to experience
the ocean is
the lover of abandonment,
Ride!
and find its tale.

Energy not brought,
not sent,
felt its way here
as it has since
before minds
made time.

From brute
to angel's whisper,
it climbs—softly,
silvery blue
with foam
to my feet
only a touch
of what
was
devastating.

                    —G.T. Young

A cold January on the North American landmass: Chicago, minus 19; South Dakota, minus 45; West Virginia, 17 inches of new snow.

Honolulu, meanwhile, at 22° N. latitude, is in the tropics but, still, well above the equator: chill winds from the southwest, a low in the low 60s—cold for here. On the south shore of Oʻahu, Venus pulses above the horizon in the postsunset sky, while at the other side of the celestial hemisphere the full moon's already up. Up, and on its feet, surfing.

Five-thirty the next morning, predawn patrol. Mercury and Jupiter up there too, full moon now in the west, apparent rate of descent accelerating as Earth approaches. "Help! Moon's falling!" Path of moonlight on the water waning as the moon, its hyper-white ever more yellow, drops closer to Planet Ocean. The sound of birds over the surf: daybreak announcing its arrival.

Full moon slipping behind gray clouds; being eaten by gray clouds; fitting like a coin into a slot of gray clouds; pulling up a mask of gray clouds to cover its eyes. Bandido moon, mouth showing through the mask. Dissing the sun: "Catch me if you can." Moonlight on the ocean almost gone. Terra firma brightening, Waiʻanae range coming into focus, pale orange moon breaking up, obscured by a smudge of cloud at the horizon in the west, now to be found only if one already knows it's there.

Six fifty-five AM. Full moon gone. Slipped away. Was here before, will return. As it did long before our genus and species arrived. As it will do long after our genus and species have themselves slipped away. Are gone.

My Hawaiʻi: a place where I try to pay attention to the physical world. No television: I watch the large screen—ocean, sky. Someone in Honolulu once asked if I was religious. "The *moana* is my religion," I responded, surprising myself. The ocean. But perhaps it was true. What a strange bargain we've made, to imagine that, say, Bill Gates and his barrage of self-promotion has something essential to offer. (My long-time acquaintance George, having given up on many aspects of American life—he has sex only in Thailand, for instance—snorts at the mania for computers. "You know what, they'll get the whole fucking universe onto a microchip," George says, laughing, "then program it to go up its own ass, and that will be end of the universe, right?")

But my Hawai'i: I've made so many returns. Once, just off the plane from San Francisco, I was all-too-soon walking around downtown, having taken the (eponymous) TheBus (sic) in from a VW repair shop out near Sand Island. My old van had further corroded while I was away, body rot, of course—so much salt air—but also disintegration of various rubber seals, a familiar problem in the tropics.

Spaced, still processing the intense foreignness of this place, having several hours to pass before the van would again be continent, I saw a woman briskly approaching, saw her almost right in front of me, in fact, before I belatedly realized I knew her well. Talk about computers! Some whole file in my mind—names/lives/identities of everyone I knew in Hawai'i—just hadn't opened yet. Opened now only with enormous effort. Brenda: she and I hadn't seen or spoken to each other for months and months, half a year or more. I'd been on the "mainland," a whole other movie. And Brenda, a lovely, witty, wry woman who now also suffered from mental illness, usually helped by and submerged under the influence of this or that powerful prescription drug, she herself was sometimes in … another whole universe.

"What are you doing here?" Brenda asked, startled. A fair question, and, given our dual disorientations, a question with quite a spin on it. What *was* I doing in Hawai'i? Once again leaving my econiche in northern California, the richness of which I'd never have time to exhaust. My friends there, knowing how hard I was to budge from the microclimate of my neighborhood, seemed still surprised I kept voyaging to the Pacific. I myself was often amazed by yet another return to Hawai'i, when even the prospect of one more transition seemed foolish, greedy, or simply a form of trying to live more than one life at a time.

And of course one returned not just to the *moana* or *kai* but to transformation of self, again a mainland *haole;* to sticker shock, experiencing a physical recoil the first time back at an island su-permarket register. The price of paradise … Also taking in the rel-ative absence of the homeless, compared to San Francisco; and the absence of mainland Black street culture, though there's plenty of crack cocaine, "ice," and violent crime in Honolulu. (Easier, by far, to uproot marijuana plants than to stop the supply of hard drugs.) Reading the morning paper, willy-nilly ingesting a sense of perva-sive bureaucratic corruption and nepotism in this one-party state; and/or the nightmarishly high incidence of domestic violence in both local and military cultures. And, out doing errands, mar-veling at such determinedly conspicuous consumption—yet an-other Rolls Royce, marble a desideratum for renovated counter-tops, bathrooms, hallways. And, in the parks, the cult of children's sports—hundreds of *keiki*s playing soccer: the centrality of family; both the love of children and/or the approved selfish selflessness of caring for kids.

Noting again the instant and endless reverbs of so small a place, every conversation born to be repeated, round and round the islands. Coconut wireless? *Sheesh, brah:* coconut internet. The banal levelings and perfidies of gossip evoking Ann Cornelisen's Italian hill villages of the early Sixties, or the Ireland Joyce and Beckett left behind. Noting also the obligatory nostalgia about the (lost) plantation past; the incessant referent of race and so many race jokes (how come no joke 'bout social class?); and the sounds of pidgin English, alternately a richly ironic, nuanced insider's lingo, also perfect for excluding outsiders, or speech intentionally dumbed down, an elective shared infantalism. All this and the achingly slow drivers, until one ... relaxes to become one of them. Settling in at eighteen, nineteen mph. Oh the trades/sun/beach/ waves/rainbows/double rainbows, termites flying at nightfall, box jellyfish ten days after the full moon, the sweet rhythms of slack key guitar, the miracle of hula. This and the pernicious financial pressure, houses costing a fortune but few being sold, realtors hunkered down for a slow "recovery," everyone working two jobs, the whole bitter joke of money in paradise. Rush hours on H-1. Cellphones proliferating, car alarms, A.A. under the banyan tree in Kapiʻolani Park, the young on scooters (no helmets/no shoes), tiny aged *tutus* walking at midday, umbrellas against the sun, off to the mall—the joy of shopping. Their impending weekend charter roundtrip to Vegas. Tourism: on some islands, two tourists for every three residents, daily. And the military—Hawaiʻi's second industry, its vast holdings of land, massive spending, nuclear presence. This, and the continued—as if intentional—dispossession of Native Hawaiians.

Soon after my arrival, there are two very public deaths. First, Hilbert Kahale Smith, about to be evicted from his home after an eighteen-year Dickensian legal struggle with the State Department of Hawaiian Home Lands, burns his house down. Smith himself never emerges from the flames, though whether or not he intended suicide is unclear. Beyond the shock of Smith's fate, however, the public issue is that there are two hundred thousand acres of land long held in trust by the state for the Hawaiian people. Remarkably, Native Hawaiians nevertheless wait generations to get a home-lot on that land; only a fraction of the land has been allocated, only a fraction of those eligible are living on it. That is, there seems to be an aggressive lack of governmental will to administer the land in favor of its intended beneficiaries. Process, process. This and a capacity for corruption that defies exposure.

The second very public death comes when John Nahale Miranda, unemployed for eight months, goes back to the company that fired him, shoots his former boss, and tapes a shotgun to the head of a former fellow worker. After many (televised-live) hours, Miranda is shot by police snipers as he's about to kill his hostage.

In its editorial, the *Honolulu Advertiser* refuses to view Miranda as a martyr, this though the Hawai'i economy is in terrible shape, though Native Hawaiians are at the bottom of the economy, and though Miranda accused his employers of having fired him for racial reasons. Several University of Hawai'i professors, however, suggest the problem is either capitalism itself and/or the political oppression of Native Hawaiians. Whatever the nexus of truths—Miranda also had a history of drug abuse—many people in Hawai'i feel great financial fear. Meanwhile, one-hundred-plus years after the overthrow of Queen Lili'uokalani, there's much talk of sovereignty for Native Hawaiians (whatever form it would take, from separate-nation status to reservation-like areas of independence, and despite the welter of competing Hawaiian groups).

Sovereignty or no, it seems to the visiting mainland *haole* that what's most remarkable in Hawai'i is the low incidence of violence by Native Hawaiians. Not against the self—there is much alcoholism and drug abuse, and the kind of crime and violence at which one gets caught, life as one fight after another. A hugely disproportionate number of Native Hawaiians in prison; high rates of infant and adult mortality and suicide; short life expectancy compared to other groups. But, still, the outsider is struck by the fact that there is no explicitly political violence. None. Or, not yet.

⌒

Scopolamine. I'm back in Hawai'i not to surf but for another dive trip, this time off the Kona—the leeward or south—coast of the Big Island of Hawai'i. Which occasions a search for the Transderm Scop (from scopolamine) patch, unfortunately, it seems, at least temporarily off the market. Somebody got sick because of it? The FDA reacted, overreacted? Production methods being revamped?

James Hamilton-Patterson writes that Cicero, who'd fled to sea "to escape Mark Antony's sentence of beheading, was so seasick he gave up and returned, preferring execution to the unconsummated death sentence passed on him by the ocean." Myself, I can endure seasickness, but now I would like to finally try the damn scopolamine patch, call a number of doctor-friends. Nope, no secret stashes. Even race car drivers, who often depend on the patch, are unable to locate any. Ah well … What is seasickness anyway, no more than a malfunction of the endolymphatic fluid in the inner ear. Too much movement, too many variables; a read of the world as stable is lost. Fatigue or an unsettled emotional state being complicating variables. And, I note in my research, women and people "with high anxiety and introverted personalities also are more vulnerable." Oneself, an introvert? Son, in any case, of a doctor committed to public service who himself was very prone to seasickness—for whom the status hunger of owning a yacht was both pathetic and biologically contra-indicated—I spend a self-prescribed half-hour each day just floating in the swell, being rocked. Tuning in; giving in.

I also take a checkup dive out in Hawai'i Kai. This comes after a restless night—cold southwest winds rattling the shoji panels—and a chilly dawn as I drive east from Diamond Head, rush-hour traffic pouring toward town on the perennially unfinished Kalaniana'ole Highway. At Vehon's dive shop, Eileen helps with gear, and soon, her husband, Don, at the helm, we're out into Maunalua Bay. A career Marine who did amphibious reconnaissance in Vietnam, having since spent years as a dive instructor, Don's well used to reading people under stress, has his own strategy for putting customers at ease when they learn to dive. And/or for testing them to read character. Blessed with total recall, Don tells jokes, non-stop: How do you stop a blonde from having sex? Why were there only five hundred Mexicans at the Alamo? An insightful man who doesn't mind being underestimated, Don watches each day's four or six divers respond to this barrage of political incorrectness. As they laugh, wince, fall silent, respond with or compete with jokes of their own. Throughout, up to the moment he anchors for the divers, one senses him calibrating the needs of this group, many of the divers usually strangers not only to him but to each other.

Divers, diving. On board, a midwesterner in medical school with his girlfriend from Toronto, who's studying at Tufts, in Boston; also a Chinese-American woman from San Francisco, graduate of U.C. Santa Cruz, who's in computers. And Don's friend Bruce, a just-retired 747 pilot, along to help out. From one dive organization alone—PADI (Professional Association of Diving Instructors), diving's General Motors—there are more than six hundred twenty-five thousand certifications for new divers each year after the mandatory classes; seventy thousand teachers at more than three thousand dive centers and resorts worldwide. The cost of the course, of the gear, of each next dive: recreational diving for the masses, big business, first pushed along in the Fifties by Cousteau's *The Silent World,* and Lloyd Bridges in *Sea Hunt.* For PADI, this means sales revenues of more than $30 million annually from marketing "an opportunity to explore a different environment ..." As John Cronin, PADI's CEO, puts it, "[Diving] defies gravity. You're flying. It's a special sport, an activity where you can touch the edge of science and adventure."

I once met a couple on Don's boat, a doctor and his professor-wife, who said they dived for the quiet. And, on the Cocos Island voyage, an Australian airline pilot and his Thai fiancée who said much the same. I believed them, but was, each time, disbelieving. All that gear, expense, technology, to get quiet? Ah, well: twentieth-century lives. So many approaches to the water. To the essential. And on this I chewed as we finished our second dive that morning in Hawai'i Kai, cold south wind still blowing, Koko Head just off to the east, Diamond Head down to the west, a boatload of Japanese tourists approaching for *their* ocean adventure.

∼

SOUND. *Noun:* the sensation produced in the organs of hearing by vibrations in air or other elastic mediums. Noise. Also, a passage of water between larger bodies of water. *Adjective:* without defect, reliable. *Verb:* To measure the depth of water by letting down a weight at the end of a line. To plunge downward or dive.

SOUNDING. *Adjective:* emitting sounds. *Noun:* the act of measuring depth or the bottom of water with a lead and line.

Getting ready for my trip: Reading. Books: keeping one afloat in the sea of life. The joy of discovering a fine writer, true and new language that leads one … deeper. Or farther from shore. Or back, finally, toward terra firma. This extraordinary ongoing conversation between writer and reader-writer and so on and on.

Poet Anne Carson, three separate lines on water (torn out of context):

> Kinds of water drown us; kinds of water do not.

> The mechanisms that keep us from drowning are so fragile: and why us?

> All at once he realizes it is not up to him, whether he drowns. Or why.

And the poet Amhairghin (fourth century BC?), coming ashore from Spain in the Celtic invasion of Ireland, declaiming,

> I am a wave of the ocean.
> I am the sound of the sea.

～

Departure time for Kona, the National Weather Service's nautical forecast for the islands offering very strong northwest winds with huge swell and surf from the north. Not so swell, really, if it wraps around to the Kona coast. *Whatevehs,* as they say in pidgin …

At the airport for the short flight, in my standard Levi's, black T-shirt, and Nike's, lugging my laptop, I'm back in the costume ball of travel and tourism. Men in green pants and white patent leather shoes—far effen out! Women in white pants wearing much of the jewelry they've earned, deserved. We seem, suddenly, like the audience of Geraldo or Oprah: *And now, live from Honolulu …*

The Big Island: black lava fields at the airport, this volcanic island very much still being born, three of its five volcanoes "active," but nonetheless with dense human history. On April 4, 1820, for instance, the Pioneer Company of the Sandwich Islands Mission arrived in the harbor at Kailua-Kona, at the foot of Hualalai, elevation some eight thousand feet. Congregational missionaries on the brig *Thaddeus,* one hundred fifty-nine days and eighteen thousand miles out of Boston, came ashore at Kamakahonu, a small cove that had been the site of Kamehameha I's home until his death the year before. Still there is Ahu'ena Heiau, a temple where the ancient *kapu* codes were overthrown by Kamehameha's son Liholiho under pressure from the widow-regent Ka'ahumanu. (The timing of the missionaries thus unbelievable: forty years after Captain Cook's landfall in Hawai'i, they arrived with the Hawaiian world in flux and available to a new state religion.) Also still there is Moku'aikaua Church, dedicated in 1837, replacing earlier thatch-roofed structures. The church has posts and beams of *'ohi'a;* pews, pulpits and railings of *koa;* walls of lava rock cemented with mortar of sand and lime from burned coral; a steeple more than one hundred feet high. All testifying to the wealth and power of the new religion.

This new religion, which became the vehicle of the conquerors. Truly, there are miracles. Witness the extraordinary recent actions of the United Church of Christ, whose missionaries were complicitous in the illegal overthrow of the Hawaiian monarchy in 1893. In 1993, the president of the church made a public apology as a first step toward reconciliation with Native Hawaiians, establishing foundations to administer grants of more than a million dollars as a form of redress. In 1996, the Church wrote, "We commit ourselves to address past and present injustices affecting Native Hawaiian people." Particularly moving are the words of The Reverend Norman Jackson:

> While this has not been an easy journey ... it has been a necessary one ... For some, this apology was much too litttle, and came much too late. For others, it was not necessary, and perhaps, offensive ... The apology was for the actions of our ancestors in the faith. Our confession is for our failure to assume responsibility for the consequence of their acts, for the reality that surrounds us now, in this very present moment ... We know reconciliation is not a hasty peace, an attempt to move forward as if there were no past ... Reconciliation calls for us to reconstruct our history ... to own the depth of the ambiguity that permeates our heritage in Hawaii.

Story. Words. The truth. Apology. Mourning. Bereavement. Collective denial; collective acknowledgement. Moving toward the end of continued injustice. Bringing the disappeared, in José Zalaquett's phrase, "out from silence." As poet Zbigniew Herbert put it, "Ignorance about those who have disappeared undermines the reality of the world." The truth does not bring the dead back to life, but getting it told in itself achieves some limited form of justice, a kind of catharsis, building of new common social memory.

～

When our dive boat leaves Kailua, we head south along the coast, the vast long flank of Mauna Loa like a horizon line running from upper left to lower right, and soon reach another locus of intense human history: mile-wide Kealakekua Bay. We anchor in the cove at Ka'awaloa, a former village site on the northern side of the bay, under three-hundred-foot cliffs of sparsely vegetated volcanic rock. Two-hundred-plus years ago, there was one death here among many, but this particular death reverberates still, a tuning fork that will not or does not or cannot stop vibrating. Kealakekua is where British captain James Cook, having "discovered" Hawai'i on his third Pacific voyage of exploration, arrived on January 16, 1779. By the morning after Cook's arrival, Gavan Daws writes, Hawaiians "came singing and shouting down to the bay in thousands. Nowhere in all his travels had Cook seen such a crowd. They swam about the ships like shoals of fish, and his men were helpless to keep them off." More than five hundred canoes, perhaps ten thousand Hawaiians. Among other things, the Hawaiians were wild for iron, stole or traded sex for nails until it seemed the ships would fall apart.

Cook, as it happened, had arrived at the start of the *makahiki* season, marked with the rising of the Pleiades, a period of freedom from taboos and restrictions for the common people, when the god Lono held sway, when Ku, god of war, was (briefly) out of season and the chiefs momentarily yielded power. Cook had arrived at Kealakekua Bay sailing clockwise around the island; *makahiki* began with a procession clockwise around the island, which ended at Kealakekua Bay. Further, the sails of the ships seemed much like the penants that were Lono's symbol. What the Hawaiians—or, what one group of Hawaiians versus another group of Hawaiians—made of all this, no one really knows.

Several weeks later, Cook's ships departed, only to quickly return to make repairs, but this arrival was less well received. When Cook rashly went ashore with a small group of marines to recover a stolen longboat, stones were thrown, shots were fired, and Cook was killed. (Was this great seaman unable to reach safety because he could not swim?)

In this story that's been so many times told and retold, and often bitterly argued—though the same limited source material is available to all readers—Cook was or was not taken to be the god Lono. Was a great Enlightenment explorer or, at fifty-one, emotionally exhausted and/or sadistic to his crew and to Natives—precursor of Joseph Conrad's Kurtz. Was or was not cannibalized by the Hawaiians, who, after his death, returned various parts from his corpse to the English.

The most recent combat concerning these events has been the dispute between Marshall Sahlins (University of Chicago) and Gananath Obeyesekere (Princeton University). Sahlins, no mean polemicist, writes that "I am seen competing favorably with Captain Cook for the title of principal villain." There are as yet no physical injuries reported in this replay of the events at Kealakekua, though some Native Hawaiian activists have dismissed the argument as simply two more *haoles* fighting about issues not their own.

History; the present. As we dive, we're just across from the white(!) obelisk commemorating Cook. Underwater: lobe coral, finger coral, plate coral, parrotfish, black longnose butterfish, bird wrasses, moray eels. All this and, one hundred ten feet down, a "monument" of piled cinderblocks echoing the obelisk above, some waggish diver's prank, but incredibly appropriate, underwater world once more with its mirror, correlative, of life on terra firma. (Waggish prank indeed: something is inscribed in the sand next to the cinderblocks underwater, decipherable only after photographer Wayne Levin develops his film. In letters composed of beer bottles reads a single word: LONO.)

"Be here now," aspiring guru Ram Dass urged in the Seventies. When we surface, two centuries after Cook, the boat's sound system is cranking out the diver's national anthem, Jimmy Buffet's

"Margaritaville." Buffet: the *t* is pronounced. His appeal? That the fan of Buffet's urban country music can take on his Anglo-Caribbean, wryly hip and world-weary hedonism, can be counted on to *really* know how to party. Buffet, along with Jacques Cousteau, the boat's spiritual exemplar. Our ship. Our space ship. An aluminum power catamaran. Length: eighty feet. Beam: twenty-eight feet six inches. Draft: five feet seven inches, that is, we can be in very shallow water. Cruising speed eighteen knots; seventeen-hundred-mile cruising range. Twenty-six hundred gallon/day freshwater makers, satellite navigation, color radar, video depth sounder, telephone, Marine band radio. Five staterooms with single and queen berths; air conditioning; private shower and head.

It was Jules Verne's Captain Nemo who, to escape tyranny on land, built his extraordinary submarine. Here, in the name of a hunger for the underwater world, we're close to shore but quite removed. In Hawai'i, so to speak—where else might we be?—but not quite. Just offshore, one might say. With all our gear, in any case, we're a triumph of industrial capitalism. A triumph of the technical and of the dollar, which alone enables such heartfelt pursuit of Nature.

Late-twentieth-century American life as, if not voyage, then (eco-) tour.

∽

Viewing. Perceiving. When we look out at the vast blue, we see not ocean, exactly, but surface: master trickster, chameleon, boundary between water and atmosphere, barrier or seal between two realities. Undulating, dancing, bending, stretching, reflecting on each side the world it faces while obscuring the other. From above, the illusion that reality remains the same as far as the mind can see,

that even the other side of the mirror is more of the familiar, if distorted. Still, what's concealed makes itself deeply felt—we know
there's more than meets the eye.

Reflection: the casting back of light after hitting a surface. *Refraction:* the change of direction of a ray of light in passing through
one medium into another. From above the shallows of the ocean
one sees objects underwater—light passes through the surface (refraction) and bounces off, say, coral (reflection) and passes back
through the surface. The refraction of light, meanwhile, alters how
the coral appears from above. Water quickly absorbs (*quenches,*
Jerry Dennis writes, in *The Bird in the Waterfall*) all but the greens
and blues—reds and yellows in the coral are not seen—and ripples
or waves on the surface bend the light. More distortion. In addition, the surface reflects what's above it. Usually the sky is blue,
gray, white, and, near shore, there may be palm trees. Thus, looking at the surface from above, one sees reflected light superim-
posed over refracted light, both images moving as the surface
moves.

Below the surface the same dynamics obtain, but here the
viewer is suspended within the refracting medium. Particularly in
shallow water, images on the underside of the surface may be
richer than above—often there are more objects to reflect. Now
coral, say, is seen on the ceiling of the under-surface as a reflection.
The light's still bent by the rippled surface, creating distortion.
There's less overlaying, but as the angle from the viewer to the surface becomes more oblique, there's a point at which the brighter
refracted light from above begins to dominate, obliterating the
reflection.

Underwater, one's also in a denser medium. Not only does

water absorb more light than does air, but minute floating parti-
cles further diffuse the light. (In shallow water, light's visible as it
streaks through the refracting medium, reflecting off these parti-
cles as it does through smoke or fog.) All of which means less vis-
ibility, and contrast—the range from highlight to shadow—is re-
duced, more so with depth.

Back at junction of water and air, the ocean never stops playing
tricks with our eyes. We can see a whale breach in calm water at,
perhaps, two miles; we see the clouds above these great volcanos at
a distance of more than one hundred miles. Or so it seems.
Mirages: *loomings*—"a coming dimly into view ... especially above
the surface, in an enlarged or distorted or indistinct form," the old
Webster's New International tells us. "Loomings," Melville titled the
first chapter of *Moby Dick*. There would be so very much for the
sailor Ishmael to see, to try to get in focus, to struggle to discern.

> Near the close of the dinosaurs' reign on land and before the first whales
> appeared in the sea, lava leaked onto the floor of the Pacific Ocean near
> the present site of the island of Hawai'i. Over the next seventy million
> years or so, more than one hundred such small fields of lava grew by re-
> peated eruptions until they reached the ocean surface to become large
> volcanic islands. Then, in time, these islands were destroyed by subsi-
> dence and erosion.
>
> —*Hawai'i Volcano Watch,*
> Wright, Takahashi,
> and Griggs

Heading south, right alongshore because the dropoff to deep blue
is so precipitous—in some places, down to six hundred feet only a
hundred yards from land. For miles we pass large swaths of black
lava flows from Mauna Loa, huge areas without vegetation, habi-
tation. Black lava, white surf, dark blue or gray sky, the huge blue/

blue-black form of Mauna Loa (13,667 feet above sea level, 18,000 feet below, apparently the largest mountain mass in the world). Sightings of dolphins or humpback whales, close enough to hear their exhalations, to see their incredibly smooth, silky passages up through the surface. South of Manuka and Pohue, we reach a series of littoral cones. One, Pu'u Hou, rising several hundred feet, was formed in the great lava flow of 1868 as the explosive encounter of lava and water ejected vast amounts of debris.

This meeting of fire and water, land being formed: truly the moment of Creation. The Big Island can unsettle—so raw, so new. One's there at the beginning, which, oddly, can suggest one's own ending. The few palms at Pohue Bay, for instance, are very cheering, two micro-oases in the immense fields of black rock.

Back in 1990, I saw the Pu'u'o'o eruption of Kilauea, then in its eighth year, as the river of lava moved through Kalapana to the ocean. The first time I approached was at night, feeling the heat well before coming over a rise and seeing the glow. The next day, I found that a black-sand beach I'd sunbathed on—in the then-obligatory state of nudity, with various aging Puna flower children—was now gone, as were many homes I'd once passed. In the same period, however, lava had added acres and acres of new land.

During the last fifteen hundred years, it turns out, nearly all the terrain of this area has been covered by lava: for Hawaiians, volcanic destruction of villages, temples, and gardens must not have been unusual. During the lifetimes of current inhabitants almost a third of the Puna district has been covered by lava. As Wright, Takahashi, and Griggs conclude, "present residents live in a lush, subtropical paradise, knowing that their land could be reclaimed by the volcano that created the paradise."

As the boat runs before the swell down the Kona coast, and when we are at anchor, I study the lava fields, the littoral cones, this boundary of lava and ocean. David Douglas, extraordinary nineteenth-century botanist and explorer, climbed Mauna Loa in 1833 and wrote, "How insignificant are the works of man in their greatest magnitude and perfection, compared with such a place. I have exhausted both body and mind, examining, measuring and performing various experiments, and now, I learn that I know nothing."

What to make of the proximity of such water, such fire, of land so unleavened? Trying to read what's right before my eyes, to take the measure of my responses, I find myself prone to an unsettling … despond. Short-term solutions? I begin to reread Pam Frierson's *The Burning Island,* dive into Kameʻeleihiwa's *Kamapuaʻa.* Ponder the indigenous gods and goddesses: of or brought to this place, a millennium or two of earned story, wisdom. I'll see what an outsider and water devotee can divine of, say, Pele, goddess of the volcano. Pele, who assumes various human forms, crone or young beauty, who made love for days to the pig-god Kamapuaʻa in *his* human incarnation, their fiery passion suggesting both archetypal play of male/female as well as the oft-hostile negotiation between the volcanic and vegetable. Pele: "Let this burn a hole into your memory," Jeanne Kawelolani Kinney has the goddess saying. "I am too busy with revisions to be stilled."

Suiting up again, another merely human metamorphosis, I remind myself that of course both fire and water can sustain, console. That, in Lee Siegel's phrase, there have been fires of love, waters of peace. *Console.* I stop, half into my wetsuit, to really hear the word, and it makes me smile: one heck of a word. *Vector, aura, root, core,* the other words it evokes. *Solace,* for instance. That is, after all's said and done, I'm a writer engaging, trying to be awake to, what I ... apprehend. Talk about oceans, or seas of lava: the magic and music of words will carry me on *their* bosomy swell. Let Emily Dickinson sing me straight(er):

> The Brain is deeper than the sea –
> For – hold them – Blue to Blue –
> The one the other will absorb –
> As Sponges – Buckets – do –
>
> The Brain is just the weight of God –
> For – Heft them – Pound for Pound –
> And they will differ – if they do –
> As Syllable from Sound –

Fire. Though my commitment to water remains undiluted, so to speak, these lava fields and littoral cones I stare at continue to disturb. Essayist Frank Stewart, writing about the volcanos of the Big Island, invokes Greek philosopher Heraclitis, whose writing survives only in fragments complicated by the possibililty that his pronouncements were intentionally cryptic. For Heraclitis, it seems, all things are interrelated, even apparent opposites; a chaotic world is in fact coherent. If change is persistent, so is a dynamic equilibrium. (Seawater, for instance, may harm humans, but is life itself for creatures of the sea.)

Further, fire is the basic constituent of all things, including, say, the soul, parts of which are, like everything else in the world at any given moment, being extinguished or rekindled. Translating

Heraclitis's elusive language, Stewart offers the term "a constant incandescing." A relentless metamorphosis: fire becoming sea, sea becoming earth and the "lightning flash"; fire living in the death of earth, air in the death of fire, water in the death of air, and earth in the death of water.

Flux? Transformation? Sun once again setting into … water? The danger for humans of their souls becoming excessively moistened: "For souls it is death to become water." (Or, as Guy Davenport renders it, "Water brings death to the psyche,") And, "Virtuous souls do not become water on the death of the body, but survive to join, eventually, the cosmic fire."

Deep diving, all this. Too deep. Deep enough to make a writer submerge to one hundred twenty feet yet one more time.

～

Moray eels. Garden eels. Green turtles. Trumpetfish, goatfish, butterflyfish, wrasses, parrotfish, surgeonfish, scorpionfish. Lobsters, octopus, the nudibranchs called Spanish Dancers. All miraculous—each an explosion of form-color-consciousness. Micro-universes, perhaps all of Creation contained in every one. Many of the divers are enchanted to see these endemic creatures, with each submersion add yet another one or two to their list. And yet, photographer Wayne Levin and I, so recently at Cocos Island, with its awesome profusion of sharks and rays, here we find ourselves having to laugh at our yearning for large pelagics. Foolish, that we're heartened even by sight of the two- to three-foot barracudas, creatures one step up in size in the food chain.

Our hunger for pelagics is compounded by frequent sightings of whales, but our boat must contend with the U.S. Marine Mammal Protection Act of 1972 and the Endangered Species Act of

1973: it's illegal to approach the whales within one hundred yards, or within three hundred yards of a cow and calf, illegal to disrupt the animals' normal behavior in any way. Though it's not illegal for the whales to approach *you*, in practice boat owners lean over backward to avoid losing their livelihood. Captain Michael, then, is not going to be dropping us overboard with the whales. So near, and yet so far.

While well-intended, these laws have the effect of precluding even swimmers from approaching the whales. No one wants boats or jet skis closing on whales. But swimmers? Famed cetacean specialist Roger Payne points out that whales can simply move away from swimmers, and that many whales, as in Scammon's Lagoon in Baja California, actively seek out the boatloads of tourists. If Payne believes humans can be saved by whales—the souls of humans, he means—he also believes human contact with whales has saved them from us. (Worldwide, some five million people went whale-watching in 1992.)

On board, then, over and again we're quite close to whales, grin to see their blows, the quick vapor-laden expulsions of air, these twenty-foot exhalations of atomized water. Smile, inadvertently, hear ourselves cheer at the sight of them breaching, or at the signature of their fifteen-foot-wide serrated flukes as they descend. Stare, silent, at the smooth slicks on the surface after they submerge, these *"pukas"* or footprints, wondering how something so vast could so suddenly be so utterly gone.

Our hunger for pelagics, particularly strong for Wayne, who's spent much time in the water over the years, usually under his own power, in kayaks and then free diving, photographing dolphins and whales in many areas of the Pacific and Caribbean.

Appealing to our own better natures, however, Wayne and I resolve to become miniaturists if necessary, for the moment to take what the gods give.

(Nature, nurture: earlier, donning gear for our first dive, Wayne and I are at the stern talking with one of the divemasters, a young woman wearing a functional and (hence?) skimpy bathing suit, whose "headlights are on," to use a phrase I encountered in an undergraduate story while teaching a few years ago. When I asked what it meant, the class laughed at my ignorance. Wayne and I, in any case, are earnestly talking water and diving, but those erect nipples are apparently part of the conversation: when Wayne and I finally jump into the water with mask, snorkel, fins, tanks, and regulators, we're unable to descend—each of us has forgotten his weight belt.)

Back at Pohue Bay, we start our afternoon dive beneath the lava cliffs, right above an underwater wall that drops down and down into the deep blue. Plan your dive and dive your plan, they say: as we again put on wet suits, weight belts, tanks, apply defogger to our masks, Wayne and I agree not to go below eighty-five feet. Soon after we descend, however, I notice that Wayne is out of my field of vision. I make a quick pivot, look above and below. Typically, Wayne has seen what there was to see and has moved toward it, fast, in this case a large black manta ray, perhaps fifteen feet across.

Rays, these flattened sharks—what a sea-change!—propelled by wings, enormous pectoral fins. Talk about aerodynamic! This beautiful black ray—white underbelly making it invisible from both below and above—seems to just hang there, moving not at all; I'm mesmerized, by its mass, form, sheer presence, by the arm-like cephalic fins on either side of its mouth. Devilfish, feeding on pearl divers, as in the old stories? No. This ray consumes planktonic crustaceans, is, for humans, no worse than an angel that's fallen through the liquid mirror of the surface.

We seem to be in a stasis, the ray and I, though I notice more than once that I'm swallowing to equalize the pressure in my ears, what a diver must do during descent. Finally, perhaps reflexively because of yet another swallow, I reach down for my depth gauge, bring it up in front of my eyes, ray just beyond. Far out—one hundred ten feet. I make a no-more-than-obligatory effort to look up, reluctantly take my eyes off the ray: ah, Wayne, ol' dive buddy, well above.

The rapture of the deep. A good part of me, without bothering to argue or even explain, seems ready, willing, able to accompany the ray. Whatever it takes. We humans have killed off countless species as a form of possession. With this creature, however, I want no trophy, but neither do I want to lose contact. The ray is not mine, that's clear, but I really do not want to let it go.

Back on board, Jack's in a state of exultation, is high, giddy. He too saw the ray. "Majestic," Jack keeps saying, "majestic." He has my sympathy: words won't suffice.

A short man of perhaps forty, Jack likes food and drink, has adjusted affably to having put on weight, walks with feet flat and out, as if the belly is of course to take the lead. He wears a T-shirt with a motif of donkeylike creatures sitting in trenches, and the message: "I'm surrounded by ass holes." Jack and his wife, who has also affably put on quite a bit of weight, are experienced divers, are bright, quick, verbal. She shows me a picture of their "son," a Boston terrier; laughs.

Seeing the domain of each marine creature—its methods of hiding, diverting, attacking, cooperating, parasitizing, attracting, repelling—one surfaces to read fellow divers here on Planet Ocean somewhat differently. That is, not, as in Cocos, to see the analogies, to make the inference—this person, for instance, too much of a shark. No, here it seems we're all just doing our thing, filling our particular ecological niche, playing out genetic roles we were dealt after eons of evolution. (In current neo-Darwinian theory, we're among the fittest of species that *by chance* happened to survive the last mass extinction.) Of various shapes, sizes, and personalities, both crew and divers are extraordinarily good natured, practice sustained self-restraint and frequent generosity in close quarters. Give middle-class styles a good name. One need not love the entire ship's company. Nonetheless, emerging to see its members after being underwater does foster a curiosity about—if not a kind of awe of—the variety of human forms that have endured.

～⌒～

Sunrise, up on deck. More whales nearby. Roger Payne on my mind:

> [Herman Melville] knew just how and by what steps whales would enter our minds, and how once inside they would metastasize and diffuse throughout the whole engine of human ingenuity, mastering and predisposing it to their purpose...that whales would reconstitute themselves, reintegrate at the point of origin of all the meridians of the imagination, its very pole, and there tie themselves forever into human consciousness by a kind of zenith knot...that when this process had completed itself the whale as symbol would have become the whale as puppeteer—would start orchestrating, manipulating, and directing the connections that people perceive between themselves and the beating heart of nature...that whales can help humanity save itself—help us to make the transition from Save the Whales to Saved by the Whales.

Could Payne be right? Could he?

～⌒～

Sunrise. Once more surveying the deep blue. The oceanic, what Marianna Torgovnick defines as "a dissolution of subject-object divisions so radical that one experiences the sensation of merging with the universe." A feeling some seek, some fear—or both.

Apropos of the Flood in the Book of Genesis, it is written, "and the waters prevailed." Also, that "the waters prevailed exceedingly." There's land here, the unstoppable, hundred-millennia-long surge of lava that raised these mountainous islands. Twenty thousand feet just to clear the surface. Still, it is also true—so few islands in so many, many square miles of ocean—still, the felt truth is that the waters do indeed seem to have prevailed.

Epilogue: The Deepener's Tale

✳

But not so deep as the deep I am in
I know not e'er I sink or swim.
                    —Trad.

DEEP. *Adjective:* extending far downward from the top, inward from the
surface, backward from the front, or far to sides or edge; covered or protected; hard to understand, profound; solemn, cunning; dark and rich;
intense; of low pitch; immersed or absorbed. *Noun:* a deep place, as in
water or earth; the extent of space or time; the unknown; the under-
world; the part that is darkest, most silent.

DEEPENER. *Noun:* one who or that which deepens.

Nineteen sixty-four to sixty-five. Cambridge, Mass. Senior year of
college, just beginning to really have the game down. Living off-
campus, away from the strictures of the neo-Oxbridge house
system. Smoking pot, for which, as I tell the nark on the plane to
Hawai'i thirty years later, one can be "expunged." Going out with a
Radcliffe student who's obsessively not writing her thesis on
Virginia Woolf, though she'll carry it off by the due date, will be
no less productive than her oft-tormented subject.

Motorcycles. Marlboros. Taking Erik Erikson's course on the Life Cycle, doing my undergraduate thesis on Conrad's *Lord Jim*. The gist of which is, why does Conrad work so hard to protect Jim by telling the story in such complex ways, by withholding information about Jim from the reader for much of the book? The story otherwise pretty simple: Jim, a romantic, fails badly, gets a second chance, fails again.

The thesis has special meaning to me. I'd come close to writing about Sir Oswald Mosley, British fascist of the Thirties, but then asked myself, why spend a chunk of my waning youth on this upper-class jerk? Unfortunately, it was really too late to change topics. And to what? But then, wandering in the subterranean stacks of Widener Library, I bumped into the Conrad section, pulled down *Lord Jim*, began to read. Changed tutors, demoted to the custody of a graduate student who, amazingly, proved as engaged in *Lord Jim* as I. Together, we set out to take Conrad's measure. Something that would have provoked Thorsten Veblen to derision: undergraduate thesis, and with meaning conspicuously consumed, no less.

Foibles of the managerial class notwithstanding, in *Lord Jim*, Marlow, the storyteller, goes to a friend, a merchant named Stein, for advice about Jim's plight. Stein says: "A man that is born falls into a dream like a man who falls into the sea. If he tries to climb out into the air as inexperienced people endeavor to do, he drowns … No! I tell you! The way is to the destructive element submit yourself, and with the exertions of your hands and feet make the deep, deep sea keep you up."

In subsequent years, I had good cause to remember the portentous language of this passage. Having gone off the deep end, I had at least as much to learn about the destructive element and my own untested dreams as Conrad or his surrogate Jim. Waist-deep in the Big Muddy, I swam like a dog, at times, to keep my head above water. Was saved, in part, by immersing myself in the sea of language, slowly making myself a writer, learning some-thing of what Henry James called "the deep countermining of art."

The deep. There's a poem by Seamus Heaney in which some Irish monks, while at prayer, behold a ship in the air above them, anchor getting hooked on the altar rails. A sailor descends the line, but can't release it. The abbot says the man will drown in this world. The monks help, the ship is freed, and the sailor is able to ascend from the realm of the "marvellous."

Various deeps, then, and the "marvellous" as I have known it. A month after seeing my Australian cousin-brother David Charles Miller and his wife and daughter in California, I received a copy of the poster they'd commissioned, from gifted painter Jasper Schreurs, for the Fiji tour of The Magic Circus of Samoa. And there, with shaved head and Fu Manchu mustache—quite unlike my own—and with many, many tattoos on arms and chest, hands both wreathed in and emanating fire, there was Bruno. As David had said, not looking a bit like me.

For those who were wondering, Richard's back in town after time in Reno and Vegas, no longer in deep shit. Finally separated from his nonwife, and bearing little resemblance to *him*self, or, more precisely, the self he's been for many years. Instead, in ap-pearance now much like the fellow I first knew in the early Seven-ties, an articulate ex-con both on the run from the law and on the college intramural basketball circuit. Free of domestic responsibil-ities, though truly missing his son, Richard's dropped seventy-five pounds and is again shooting hoops, compares himself favorably to—sure sign of self-deception—himself when younger.

As for Ann, in whose dazzlingly overgrown home I was asked about my trip to Samoa—with many of her friends Ann has gone quite silent recently: still waters can run very deep.

Regarding the nark on the plane as I headed to Samoa via Honolulu: if you see him, let him know I recently attended a party in Palolo Valley in Honolulu, the night warm, soft, moist; fecund. Brazilian drummers, palms flying, setting a cadence with which one, finally, could only resonate, guests at last not so much dancing as vibrating in place. The pipe of *paka lolo*—Hawaiian pot, very strong—making the rounds yet again, again, again. Perhaps, I thought, smiling to see the moon through the clouds as if it were a long-lost friend, perhaps I *had* been overdoing abstinence.

The marvelous: this body of mine—not to make too much of it—which has served me (or us, if mind *&* body are in it together) so well. Still, somewhere in *its* deeps is the formula describing which part will need repair, which part will cease to persist when— in which room the domestic terrorist's bomb will explode. What will put me in, to take a phrase from "Wake Up Little Suzy," *trouble deep.*

Childhood, before I first heard the Everly Brothers. Long since, my childhood seems improbably long ago. I remember, I remember more than one Christmas Eve caroling at Louisburg Square on Beacon Hill with my mother and my siblings. Singing: "Good King Wenceslaus looked out, on the feast of Stephen." Nudging my brother—Stephen was, is, his name. "When the snow lay round about, deep and crisp and even."

William Blake's "fathomless *&* boundless deep,/There we wander, there we weep …" Rocked in the cradle of the deep. Of language, of story. This book: writing, rewriting, fall become winter become spring become … Dreaming these stories long before I could see them; wondering, often, where I was bound, yet another voyage out.

Art; magic. Time to break my staff, as Prospero put it in *The Tempest,* to "Bury it certain fadoms in the earth,/And deeper than did ever plummet sound/I'll drown my book." *Drown my book?*

What Hamilton-Patterson calls time's liquid correlative. In the years (?) left to me, I hope for rideable waves, the sweet deep calm of morning glass. And, as someone who has more than once been caved by warm oceans, let me reiterate, before the fact, a last request: when I die, please, cast my ashes upon, yes, the face of the deep.

Credits

Amhairghin, translated by Proinsias MacCana in *Celtic Mythology* (Hamlin Publishing Group, a division of Reed International Books, 1968), as cited in Thomas Cahill's *How the Irish Saved Civilization* (Doubleday, 1993).

Ammons, A.R., from "Swells," in *A Coast of Trees* (W.W. Norton, 1981).

Calvino, Italo, from *Invisible Cities,* translated by William Weaver (Harcourt, Brace & Jovanovich, 1974).

Carson, Anne, from *Plainwater: Essays and Poetry* (Alfred A. Knopf, 1995).

Dening, Greg, from *Islands and Beaches* (Honolulu: University of Hawai'i Press, 1980), and from *Mr. Bligh's Bad Language* (Cambridge University Press, 1992).

Heaney, Seamus, from "Settings" in Seeing Things (Noonday Press, Farrar, Straus & Giroux, 1991).

Jabès, Edmond, translated by Rosmarie Waldrop, from *The Little Book of Unexpected Subversion* (Stanford University Press, 1996) and from *The Book of Questions,* vols. 1 and 2 (Wesleyan University Press, 1991).

Larkin, Philip, from "The Old Fools," in *High Windows* (Farrar, Straus & Giroux, 1974).

Pi'ilani, translated by Frances N. Frazier, from "The True Story of Kaluaiko'olau, or Ko'olau the Leper," *The Hawaiian Journal of History,* vol. 21, 1987.

Stewart, Susan, from *On Longing* (Johns Hopkins University Press, 1984).

About the Author

© *Wayne Levin*

Awarded Guggenheim and National Endowment fellowships for fiction and creative nonfiction, Thomas Farber has been Visiting Distinguished Writer at the University of Hawaiʻi, Fulbright Scholar for Pacific Island Studies, recipient of the Dorothea Lange–Paul Taylor Prize, and Rockefeller Foundation resident scholar at Bellagio. His many books include *On Water, Learning to Love It,* and, with photographer Wayne Levin, *Through a Liquid Mirror.* He is currently Visiting Senior Lecturer at the University of California, Berkeley.